The Asian Literature Bibliography Series

GUIDE TO
CHINESE POETRY AND DRAMA

The Asian Literature Program
of The Asia Society

General Editor

Guide to

CHINESE POETRY
and DRAMA

ROGER B. BAILEY

G. K. HALL & CO.
70 LINCOLN STREET, BOSTON, MASS.
1973

Z
3108
L5 B3

Copyright © 1973, by G. K. Hall & Co.

All Rights Reserved

Library of Congress Cataloging in Publication Data

Bailey, Roger B.
  Guide to Chinese poetry and drama.
  (The Asian literature bibliography series)
    1. Chinese poetry—Bibliography. 2. Chinese drama—Bibliography. I. Title.
II. Title: Chinese poetry and drama. III. Series.
Z3108.L5B34   016.8951'1'008   73-11462
ISBN   0-8161-1102-2

Acknowledgment

The "Key to Chinese Pronunciation" is reprinted from *The Travels of Lao Ts'an*, by Liu T'ieh-yün, translated by Harold Shadick. Copyright 1952 by Cornell University. Used by permission of Cornell University Press.

MANUFACTURED IN THE UNITED STATES OF AMERICA

CONTENTS

201916

FOREWORD

This annotated bibliography series on Asian literature was initiated in response to the needs of the nonspecialist. It is hoped that the summaries and evaluations to selected works available in translation together with the general introduction in each guide to the literature under examination will aid educators and students on both the secondary and college level as well as the general reader and those in institutions who want to build up responsibly their collection of Asian writings. Although compiled for an audience completely unfamiliar with Asian literature, these guides are also intended to be reference works for students and scholars exploring a particular subject. In addition, they should benefit those in disciplines other than literature—Asian heritage studies, anthropology, history, philosophy, the social sciences—who wish to take advantage of translated literature as a rich source of material for their studies. Books that are not available in libraries may be ordered through the publishers or through such specialized bookstores as Paragon Book Gallery, New York, Hutchins Oriental Books, California, or The Cellar Book Shop, Michigan.

Naturally, each author has his own criteria for the way the material in his guide is selected, presented, and judged. However, the intent of the author has been to indicate clearly and honestly the range and artistic merit of all the titles annotated and thereby guide the reader to those specific works which will satisfy his scholarly and aesthetic needs.

Arranged by topic and chronology, each guide covers the translated literature from the earliest times to today, but none pretend to be comprehensive. In most cases, works that are not recommended or have been superseded by better versions have been excluded. Omitted also are very specialized studies and inaccessible translations (thus excluding much of what has appeared in magazines and journals), and a number of translations which are too new to have been included in the guides. This increase in translation activities is a welcome sign. It points to a growing awareness of the importance of listening to Asian voices (rather than only to Western interpreters of

Asia) and to the growing recognition of the place of Asian writings in world literature and of the place of translators in the creative field. Hopefully, these guides will serve the reader who later turns to translations not annotated or discussed here.

A series of this scope required the involvement of a number of people. I would especially like to thank the authors who have prepared these guides and the many scholars who have acted as consultants throughout the preparation of each manuscript, offering invaluable suggestions and criticism. Acknowledgment is also due Junnko Tozaki Haverlick of the Asian Literature Program of The Asia Society under whose editorial guidance these guides were prepared.

BONNIE R. CROWN, Director
The Asia Society   *Asian Literature Program*

Key to Chinese Pronunciation

Most Chinese "words" or names consist of from one to three syllables. The generally accepted system of transliterating Chinese used in the English-speaking world is the Wade-Giles system. Most of the syllables are represented in this system as consisting of two parts, an initial consonant and a final vowel or vowel group (sometimes ending in *n* or *ng*). Ten finals (*a, ai, an, ang, ao, e* or *o, en, ou, i, erh*) can form syllables without initials. The following tables show approximately how the Wade-Giles symbols should be pronounced.

INITIALS

Wade-Giles Symbol	Pronounced	Wade-Giles Symbol	Pronounced
ch	j in jay	p'	p in spill
ch'	ch in charm	s	s
f	f	sh	sh
h	h (slightly guttural)	ss or sz (only used before u)	s
hs	sh	t	d
j	r	t'	t
k	g in gay	ts	dz
k'	k in skill	ts'	ts
l	l	tz (only before u)	dz
m	m	tz' (only before u)	ts
n	n	w	w in way
p	b in bait	y	y in you

FINALS

Wade-Giles Symbol	Pronounced	Wade-Giles Symbol	Pronounced
a	ah	ia	yah
ai	eye	iang	yahng
an	on in yon, or ann in mann (German)	iao	yow (ow in how)
		ieh	yeah
ang	in lang (German)	ien	yen
		ih	rr (not trilled)
ao	ow in how		
e or ê	u in cup	in	in
ei	ay in say		
en or ên	un in bun	ing	ing
eng or êng	ung in bung	iu	ew in mew
		iung	ee + ung, or jung (German)
erh or êrh	er in ermine		

Wade-Giles Symbol	Pronounced	Wade-Giles Symbol	Pronounced
i (sometimes written yi when there is no other initial)	ee	o (after initials other than h and k)	aw in law
o (after h and k or without initial)	u in cup	uang	oo + ang in lang (German)
ou (ow)	ow in low	ui (wei)	way
		un	un in und (German)
u (after initials other than ss or sz, tz, tz')	oo	ung	ung in bung (German)
u or ŭ or e (after ss or sz, tz, tz')	indicates prolonged buzz produced by voicing the consonant	uo	uaw in squaw
		ü	ü in über (German)
ua	wa in wand, or ua in guava	üan	ü + ann in mann (German)
uai	wi in wine	üeh (io)	ü + eah in yeah, or ue in luette (French)
uan	wan, or uan in Don Juan (Spanish)	ün	une (French)

A FEW EXAMPLES OF COMPLETE SYLLABLES

Wade-Giles	Components	Complete Syllable as in
so	s + o	saw
lao	l + ao	(al)low
tao	t + ao	Dow
t'eng	t' + eng	tongue
T'ieh	t + ieh	(twen)ty hei(rs)
Liu	l + iu	(loca)l u(nion) or lieu
Ts'an	ts' + an	(i)t's Hon(duras)
ying	y + ing	(pla)ying
yün	y + ün	(cit)y un(ion)

NOTE TO THE READER

Chinese names are rendered in their Chinese order—the family name first, followed by the personal name. Commas dividing last and first names have been used only where there might be cause for confusion. Cross-reference numbers in parentheses refer to entry numbers, not page numbers, unless otherwise indicated.

INTRODUCTION: POETRY

This introduction is not an outline history of Chinese poetry. The last section of the bibliography refers the reader to a number of works that give at least a respectable overall view of this vast subject, so unnecessary duplication of what can be had elsewhere will be avoided. The bibliography addresses itself to those who are approaching the study of Chinese poetry for the first time. Individually, the annotations describe and make judgments on specific works. Taken as a whole, however, the bibliography should enable the reader to acquire as good a fundamental knowledge of Chinese poetry as is available to the English-speaking reader. This introduction, a guide to the bibliography, surveys some landmarks in the history of Chinese poetry through collected works, individual poets, simple works, or poetic types. The few translations included as examples of points made in the text are my own. They do not intend to be elegant; they can only hope to be accurate. If the introduction and bibliography help the beginning student to get his bearings, they will have served their purpose adequately.

The *Book of Songs* (*Shih ching*) is the oldest collection of Chinese poetry. According to one Chinese tradition, Confucius (551-479 B.C.) compiled this anthology from some three thousand ancient poems. However, most modern scholars believe that the *Book of Songs* came down to him in much the same form that it has come down to us and that his main function was that of transmitter. Certainly his name is inseparably linked with the *Book of Songs*, if for no other reason than that he so consistently advocated the study of it. Several times in the *Analects* (*Lun Yü*), a book of sayings attributed to Confucius and probably written down by a disciple, he urges his disciples to learn the *Songs:* "Why should you my disciples not study the *Songs?* They stir the spirits, they improve one's perceptions, they teach you how to get along with others, they show you how to get angry without flying into a rage. They lead one from the knowledge of how to serve one's father to the knowledge of how to serve one's ruler. They also increase one's familiarity with the names of birds, animals, plants and trees." Confucius' great esteem for these songs also accounts in large part for the jealous care with which they have been preserved down through the centuries.

The 305 songs are divided into three unequal parts: 160 folk songs (*feng*), 105 court songs (*ya*), and 40 sacrificial songs (*sung*). Actually, these English translations for the words *feng*, *ya*, and *sung* only approximate the original, and while there seems to be no violent controversy over this principle of classification, neither is there any consensus. The *feng* songs seem to have come from thirteen ancient Chinese states. Although their stylistic uniformity suggests that they were reworked by a single editor or group of editors (some would say Confucius himself), their subject matter indicates a folk origin. The *ya* songs include some dynastic legends that may seem appropriate to the court, but there are also a number of songs similar to those in the *feng* group. The *sung* songs are doubtless the oldest in the collection. Perhaps dating from before 1000 B.C., they have less value as literature than as source material for ancient religious belief and practice. Of the three groups, the *feng* songs have been the most read and have the greatest immediacy and charm. Some songs, meant to be sung at work, are rhythmical and, at times, even onomatopoeic. Other songs describe the lives of the people, their loves and courtships, their griefs and hardships, their fears and longings. The first song in the collection, even in an extremely literal translation, may be cited as a particularly fine example of the simple directness that characterizes so much of the *Book of Songs:*

> "Kuan Kuan" the fish hawks
> On the river island;
> Retiring, refined, the virtuous maid,
> A good mate for the prince.
>
> Uneven the floating *hsing* plant.
> Left and right she seeks it;
> Retiring, refined, the virtuous maid,
> Waking and sleeping he seeks her,

Seeks her to no avail.
Waking and sleeping he thinks of her,
Longing, yearning
Tossing and turning.

Uneven the floating *hsing* plant,
Left and right she picks it;
Retiring, refined, the virtuous maid,
With lute and lyre he charms her.

Uneven the floating *hsing* plant,
Left and right she gathers it;
Retiring, refined, the virtuous maid,
With bell and drum he delights her.

This song illustrates some of the features of the *Book of Songs* as a whole. The translation perhaps does not represent the characteristic four-word line, but it does follow the ballad-like refrain with the repetition and incremental repetition. It is also like many other songs in the collection in that its subject is love; the stages of finding, picking and gathering or selecting the *hsing* waterplant parallel the stages of a courtship. The song is not at all explicit, but while there is room for difference of opinion regarding its interpretation, taken literally, it must be a love song, and this fact was the stumbling block to early Confucianists. How could Confucius have advocated the study of love songs? Obviously, he could not have, they thought: there must be ethical meanings beneath the frivolous surface. As a result, since the Han dynasty (206 B.C.-A.D. 220), editions of the *Book of Songs* have been encumbered with such an oppressive load of moralistic and political commentary that the songs themselves have been all but obscured. Its status as a Confucian classic has ensured the preservation of the *Book of Songs*, but it has rarely contributed to its understanding. However, there have always been some enlightened readers who have seen the *Book of Songs* for what it is. A few poets have even attempted imitations of its four-word line, but they have not generally been successful. As highly prized as this first collection has always been, it did not greatly influence subsequent Chinese poets who preferred the greater freedom and variety of five- or seven-word lines to the restriction and even possible monotony of four.

The second great collection that has come down to us is the *Ch'u Tz'u* or *Songs of Ch'u* The most important of these songs have been traditionally attributed to Ch'ü Yüan (fl. fourth century B.C.), who is often called the father of Chinese poetry. He is well remembered for his unswerving loyalty to his state and ruler, and for his poetry, which embodies his high principles. He was an advisor to the king, but it was his misfortune to be slandered and to fall from favor. The exact details of this episode are not known, but legend says that after Ch'ü Yüan's native Ch'u fell to the state of Ch'in, in his grief, Ch'ü Yüan drowned himself. The Dragon Boat Festival, on the fifth day of the fifth month, commemorates his death.

The most considerable poem in the *Songs of Ch'u* is the "Li Sao" or "Encountering Sorrow," one of the longest poems in Chinese literature. Its 375 lines are, broadly speaking, a birth-to-death account of a virtuous man's spiritual journey; an allegorical treatment of Ch'ü Yüan's own assiduous cultivation of righteousness and the rejection and disillusionment with which he was rewarded. There are two important metaphors in the "Li Sao" which are necessary to its understanding. The first is the imagery of flowers and weeds. The poet speaks of having decked himself with orchids, and the poem abounds with names of exotic flowers that collectively seem to indicate the poet's virtues. The weeds, of course, refer to the corrupt enemies who have slandered the poet before his sovereign: "I grieve that fragrant flowers grow amidst patches of weeds." The second metaphor is that of the lover and his fickle mistress and represents Ch'ü Yüan and his sovereign. Actually, this metaphor is peculiarly suited to Ch'ü's situation; the king, the embodiment of his country, has been led to doubt Ch'ü Yüan's loyalty, just as a mistress might be led to doubt her lover's fidelity. The allegorical quest for a beauty who will be faithful ends in apparent disillusionment when the poet decides to follow in the path of P'eng Hsien, the legendary minister of remote antiquity, who drowned himself because of his sovereign's heedlessness.

One of the most interesting—and perplexing—of the poems in the *Ch'u Tz'u* is the "T'ien Wen" or "Heavenly Questions." The entire poem (about two hundred lines) consists of rhymed riddles or questions about the creation of the world, the universe, and the early history of China. The questions are rarely answered in the poem. Several can be answered from surviving traditions; the answers to the rest remain unknown. However, it is fairly certain that Ch'ü Yüan's contemporaries knew the answers to all of them. Even though we can only make conjectures as to the purpose of the work, it is still invaluable as a fairly reliable source of myths and legends current in Ch'ü Yüan's time. With certain allowances, the "T'ien Wen" can be seen as the Chinese equivalent of Hesiod's *Theogony*; its 170 questions seem to approach a systematization of early myths and legends.

The verse form characteristic of the *Ch'u Tz'u* has been ably discussed by Watson, Hightower, and especially Hawkes (nos. **46, 79, 32,** respectively). It is enough to say here that the verse form of the *Songs of Ch'u* represents an expansion of the restrictive four-syllable-line poetry of the *Book of Songs* and suits its narrative and descriptive purposes. This later verse form, unlike that of *Book of Songs,* exerted considerable influence on later Chinese poetry; it had a direct influence on the *fu* (prose poetry) and at least an indirect influence on the five-syllable *shih* (verse of uniform line length) of the Han dynasty (206 B.C.-A.D. 220).

The *fu,* variously translated as "prose poetry" or "rhyme-prose," seems to be a direct development from the *Ch'u Tz'u.* Indeed, some of the earliest specimens of *fu* are imitations of the *Ch'u Tz'u* in form and content. A good example is the "Lament for Ch'ü Yüan" by Chia Yi (201-169 B.C.), translated by Burton Watson in *Anthology of Chinese Literature* (no. **22**). The main difference between this early example and the later *fu* is in the tendency of later *fu* to be written in alternating prose and verse; even the short *fu* poems of the post-Han period (especially 221-264) usually had at least a prose introduction. The early *fu* poems like Chia Yi's are lyrical or narrative or both and do not present insurmountable obstacles to the translator. The *fu*, however, is almost impossible to translate in those works that are most characteristic of the genre. It is small wonder that the greatest practitioner of *fu* poetry, Ssu-ma Hsiang-ju (179–117 B.C.) has rarely been presented to the world in English, although several of his works have appeared in German. Easily the best translations from Ssu-ma Hsiang-ju are to be found in Burton Watson's *Records of the Grand Historian of China* (no. **45**).

The *fu* especially lends itself to high-flown descriptions of magnificent buildings, cities, and landscapes. It was a form most suitable for celebrating the grandeur of a great dynasty, but because of its extreme artificiality in structure and language, it has not enjoyed a place in the mainstream of Chinese poetry. The later *fu* tends to become a kind of balanced lyrical prose with only a tenuous connection to the *fu* of the Han dynasty.

Of considerable greater importance than the *fu* to the later development of Chinese poetry is the *shih*, or verse of uniform line length, at first consisting of five syllables to a line and later seven. These early *shih* had no set overall length. Speculations on how the five-syllable *shih* developed are beyond the scope of this introduction. It will be enough to say that *shih* poetry began to be the dominant verse form towards the end of the Han dynasty, perhaps under the impetus of folk poetry (folk poetry was at least a factor in its development), and has continued to be so in an unbroken tradition of two thousand years. Notable among the early specimens of *shih* are the simple and poignant "Nineteen Old Poems" and the narrative poem "Southeast the Peacock Flies," both translated by Payne and Waley (in nos. **13, 8**). The latter is a long poem recounting the tragedy of a young wife who is sent away by a cruel mother-in-law. Her husband vows to be reunited with her, but before he can carry out his plans, she is forced to marry an official. Unable to be together in life, the two commit suicide, she by drowning and he by hanging. As in *Romeo and Juliet*, which the story superficially resembles, the lovers are buried together. The boughs of two trees planted as a memorial intertwine.

The greatest writer of *shih* poetry before the great poetic flowering of the T'ang dynasty (618-907) was T'ao Ch'ien, or T'ao Yüan-ming (365-427), to use the style name by which he is known to the Western world. Because of the simplicity of T'ao's language, his infrequent allusions, and the universality of his themes, his work perhaps offers the best initiation into Chinese poetry. His desire to escape the hectic—indeed, in his day, perilous—life of officialdom and retreat to the country as a simple farmer is a theme frequently found in Western literature. It is a basic motivation behind such works as Vergil's *Ecologues*, Sidney's *Arcadia*, and much of Wordsworth's poetry. T'ao's work has, in fact, been compared to Wordsworth's, particularly because love of nature figures so prominently in both. Although he reveals himself through his poetry, he is perhaps best approaced through his autobiographical sketch entitled "Mr. Five Willows"; other poems that deal with the joys of simple pastoral living are "Returning to Live on the Farm," "Passing Ch'ü-a," and "Returning Home" (all translated in Payne, Acker, and Chang-Sinclair, nos. **13, 41, 42**). The first of two short lyrics on "Moving" is surely the most concise statement of T'ao's aspirations:

> From of old I have wanted to live in South Village
> But not because of any auspiciousness in its dwellings:
> I have heard that there were many men of pure heart
> With whom it would delight me to pass mornings and evenings.
> I have wished this for some years now,
> And today I am taking the step.
> There is no need for a spacious cottage;
> A mat and a bed should be quite enough.
> The neighbors will often come by,
> And freely we will chat about the past;
> We'll find our pleasure in wondrous literature
> And resolve one another's doubts.

T'ao Ch'ien's most celebrated piece, "Peach Blossom Fountain" (in nos. **13, 42, 22**), tells of a fisherman who, having lost his way, comes upon a race of men who have separated themselves from the outside world. They have created for themselves an ideal way of life and they invite the fisherman to join them. He stays awhile but soon decides to leave, thinking that he will be able to return with his friends. His attempts to retrace his steps to this golden age of civilization are unavailing, and no one has gone there since. "Peach Blossom Fountain," then, might be read as an allegory of T'ao Ch'ien's own longings for an ideal existence untroubled by the hubbub of the world.

One of the significant contributions of T'ao Ch'ien's age, the four hundred years separating the end of the Han dynasty from the beginning of the T'ang, was in literary criticism. The first piece of literary criticism, "A Discussion about Literature" (in no. **38**), was written by Ts'ao P'ei (187-226). In this short piece, the author sets forth his celebrated dicta on *ch'i*, or inspiration, and on poetry as perpetuation. Later, Lu Chi (261-303) concerned himself in his "Essay on Literature" (nos. **37-40**) with the philosophy of composition. Liu Hsieh (ca. 465-522), in *The Literary Mind and the Carving of Dragons* (no. **43**), concentrated on the description of the literary genres, a topic barely touched on by Ts'ao P'ei and Lu Chi. Another influential literary critic of this period was Shen Yüeh (441-513). Shen Yüeh, who was also a poet, has the distinction of having defined the four tones in the Chinese language of his day. On the basis of his findings, he laid down certain rules which he thought should govern the writing of poetry. Although there were four tones in Chinese, they were of two types; *p'ing*, or even, and *tse*, or uneven. Shen Yüeh's regulations, to simplify somewhat drastically, call for a balancing of even and uneven tones in certain couplets, as in the following:

> *p'ing p'ing tse tse p'ing*
> *tse tse p'ing p'ing tse*

It was the belief of Shen Yüeh and his followers that such a practice would exploit the musical potentialities of Chinese to the fullest. One may well join Shen Yüen's many critics in asking how he could then explain the successes of Chinese poetry before his time. What later became of it is a matter of record, and while it seems that Shen's influence should have been damaging, this is by no means the case. In the hands of doggerel versifiers and poetasters, his rules were of little use, but "regulated verse" (*lü shih*), as it came to be called, written by masters like Tu Fu (712-770), was one of the glories of T'ang literature; indeed, it is probably the outstanding literary product of the T'ang dynasty, much as the sonnet, which it resembles, is the greatest poetic achievement of sixteenth-century England.

In addition to the foremost consideration of the intricate tonal pattern, there are these additional requirements: same rhyme throughout, generally falling on even-numbered lines; five or seven syllables (words) to a line; eight lines in the poem; and a pattern of verbal parallelism, illustrated by the following pairs of lines from a poem by Li Po:

> Green Hills traverse northern suburbs
> White water circle eastern city
>
> Floating cloud wandering one's thoughts
> Sinking sun old friend's feelings

Obviously, poets before Shen Yüeh employed many of these same devices, but never before had they been set up as a definite set of regulations. In the T'ang dynasty, then, "regulated" or "new-style" verse existed side by side with what was called "old-style" verse, or verse that did not observe the regulations; T'ang poets excelled in both. Of the more than two thousand poets of the T'ang whose names and works are known to us, we can look briefly here at only four: Wang Wei, Li Po, Tu Fu, and Po Chü-i. They have traditionally been regarded as the greatest T'ang poets and certainly they have received more attention from Western scholars than have any of their contemporaries.

Wang Wei (669-759) is best known as a nature poet. He was also a painter, and it has frequently been said that there was painting in his poetry and poetry in his painting. His paintings, unfortunately, have not survived even though he did leave a valuable treatise on the subject. It is true that his poems are paintings; it is characteristic of his art that he is able, in one or two lines of verse, to evoke a landscape. He is like Wordsworth, interested not only in nature as it appears to the eye, but nature as man unites himself to it in mystical harmony. In fact, much of his poetry expresses the Zen Buddhist's wish to escape from the world. Wang Wei excelled in the poetic form known as *chüeh-chü* ("stop-short verse"), a regulated verse in four lines. The following poem has often been quoted to illustrate his word-painting:

> White rocks jut out from Ching Stream;
> Weather is cold and red leaves are few.
> No rain falls on the mountain pathway,
> But green mist dampens my robes.

Wang Wei has been translated quite frequently and can be sampled in Bynner-Kiang and Payne as well as in Chang-Walmsley (nos. **47, 13, 52**).

Li Po (701-762) is the best-known of Chinese poets, in or out of China; the poetic results he achieves are at times almost sublime. His life was as unconventional as his muse was untrammeled, and legends about him are almost as familiar to the Chinese as are his poems. Drinking wine seems to have been Li Po's favorite occupation. While other poets, like T'ao Ch'ien, wrote of wine as a source of good fellowship and as a means of escaping sorrows, Li Po regarded it as a source of poetic inspiration. Lovely women and friendship are two other important themes in Li Po's poetry; some of his most moving poems are those on separation from friends. Surely few poets have so successfully evoked the melancholy of parting.

A certain otherworldliness in Li Po's poetry has made him "The Poetic Immortal." His younger contemporary Tu Fu (712-770), the greatest of Chinese poets, has been called "The Poetic Sage." These titles point up Li Po's apparent lack of restraint as opposed to the conscientious craftsmanship of Tu Fu. In contrast to Li Po's preoccupations with wine, women, and the flight of poetic imagination, is Tu Fu's traditionally Confucian love for family and friends, extending to mankind in general and to common people in particular. Tu Fu lived in troubled times when thousands of poor men were sent away from their homes to fight and die. Indeed, he suffered himself not a little, and a profound sympathy for humanity is perhaps the distinctive characteristic of his poetry. His deep experience of his times and his keen observations of them have made his poetry indispensable source material for any study of the T'ang dynasty. He excelled in all the poetic forms of his day, but his "regulated verse" poems are especially treasured.

In later life, Wang Wei retired from official life to a life of contemplation; Li Po was never really temperamentally suited to a position of much responsibility. Tu Fu had been trained for official life, but his verse reflects his failure to gain advancement—or even make a decent living. Po Chü-i (772-846), on the other hand, was an official all his life and, in spite of a few reverses, rose quite high in office. Like Tu Fu, Po Chü-i was a Confucian and conceived of poetry as having a moral function. A number of his poems, such as "The Charcoal Seller" (in nos. **13, 8**), are undisguised social protest. He is best known, perhaps, for the two long poems that were included in *The Three Hundred T'ang Poems* (nos. **47-49**): "A Song of Unending Sorrow" and "The Song of a Guitar." "A Song of Unending Sorrow" celebrates the famous T'ang Emperor Ming who, a quarter of a century before Po Chü-i was born, had loved the beautiful concubine Yang Kuei-fei. Because of a revolt against her that was beyond the emperor's control, she had been put to death. She in death and he in life could only know the unending sorrow of separation. This story has been treated by a number of Chinese writers, notably Ch'en Hung, Po Chü-i's contemporary, who wrote a prose version of the story, and Hung Sheng, whose dramatic version, *The Palace of Eternal Youth* (no. **98**), was written near the end of the seventeenth century.

Some of the greatest Chinese poetry was written during the T'ang dynasty, and the remarkable productivity of the period (some fifty thousand poems have survived) is partly due to the prosperity of the age itself and the imperial patronage enjoyed by so many poets. Because of its large number of poets of the first rank, the T'ang dynasty can be compared with the English Renaissance; even more striking in both ages were the many poets whom we consider minor only because they have been obscured by such brilliant figures as Shakespeare and Spenser, Li Po and Tu Fu.

The last development in traditional Chinese poetry that will concern us here, *tz'u* poetry, began to appear during the last years of the T'ang dynasty; but, because it was perfected in the Sung dynasty (960–1279), it has been considered a contribution—perhaps the outstanding contribution—of the Sung. *Shih* poetry is characterized by a generally rigid uniformity of line length; *tz'u* poetry, on the other hand, is characterized by uneven line length. It is by no means "free verse," however, because the length of the lines, the rhyme scheme, the tonal pattern, and the length of the poem are determined by the music to which the *tz'u* is set. One speaks in Chinese of "composing" *shih*, but of "filling in" *tz'u* because a *tz'u* is a set of words fitted to a preexisting tune. While most of the original songs have long since been lost, hundreds of lyric patterns still survive. *Tz'u* poems normally go under the name of the original tune to which they were written, and have as little in common with the original words themselves as the Christmas song "What Child is This?" has with the verse compliment to "Lady Greensleeves." The *Anthology of Chinese Literature*, edited by Cyril Birch (no. **22**), gives the names of the original tunes in its selection of fifty *tz'u*; Glen Baxter has translated nine *tz'u* by the ninth-century poets Wen T'ing-yün and Wei Chuang, all set to the tune "Strangers in Saint's Coif." The rendering is so skillful that they all actually look alike on the page. "Strangers in Saint's Coif" is an extremely common tune pattern: the first two lines contain seven syllables and the remaining six lines each contain five syllables—its rhyme scheme is *AA BB CC DD*. Like many other *tz'u*, these revolve around love and beautiful women. Another theme, loneliness, is treated by a much later poet, Hsin Ch'i-chi (1140–1207), in still another poem set to "Strangers in Saint's Coif":

> The waters of Clear River flow beneath the Terrace of
>   Sorrowful Loneliness;
> In their midst how many are the tears of travelers?
> I gaze toward Ch'ang-an in the northwest
> And regret that there are so many mountains.
> But the green mountains are not able to hold back the river
> Which still flows on eastward.
> This evening on the river saddens me—
> In the deep mountains I hear the cries of partridges.

The life and work of Su Tung-p'o (1037-1101), the greatest poet of the Sung dynasty, have been excellently presented in a biography by Lin Yutang and a selection of translations by Burton Watson (nos. **75, 66**), as well as in general collections of *tz'u* like the anthology already mentioned and Mrs. Candlin's *Herald Wind* (no. **62**). The most celebrated member of a great literary family, Su Tung-p'o was an extraordinarily versatile man of letters and one of the foremost essayists in Chinese literature. He enjoyed unusual honors in all of his examinations and exhibited considerable promise as a career official, but he constantly encountered difficulties with powerful enemies and spent large portions of his life in exile. It was during one of these exiles that he composed two of his most notable works, the wonderful "Prose Poems (*fu*) on Red Cliff."

This introduction should not end without some mention of *ch'ü*, a poetic form not unlike *tz'u*, which came to be the vehicle for arias in traditional Chinese drama. Good examples of this form are to be found in two Yüan dynasty (1279-1368) plays included in the Birch anthology (no. **22**) and Henry Hart's translation of *The Western Chamber* (no. **96**).

The modern age has not produced poetry of the first rank. In the first part of this century there was a strong tendency towards the vernacular. This movement was an extremely healthy one for fiction and drama, both of which had always been written in the vernacular, because it brought to the fore the high literary worth of these formerly despised literary forms. Chinese poetry written in everyday speech, however, is long-winded in contrast to the literary language: it lacks the evocative quality, the suggestive power of the best traditional poetry. In spite of this, it is perhaps premature to make final judgments on a tradition scarcely half a century old.

ANNOTATED BIBLIOGRAPHY

General Anthologies

1. Cranmer-Byng, L., tr. *A Lute of Jade: Selections from the Classical Poets of China*. London: John Murray, 1909. 112 pp. (Paperback, Paragon Book Reprint Corp.).
2. ———. *A Feast of Lanterns*. London: John Murray, 1916. 95 pp. (Paperback, Paragon Book Reprint Corp.).

These two volumes together contain some one hundred fifteen poems, primarily of the T'ang (618-907) and Sung (960-1279) dynasties. *A Lute of Jade* includes five or six pre-T'ang poems and *A Feast of Lanterns*, a dozen post-Sung poems by the notable Ch'ing dynasty (1644-1911) poet Yüan Mei (1715-1797). The introductions to both volumes are of a rather miscellaneous nature and show considerably more zeal than knowledge. The beginner should read them in the light of more recent authoritative studies because they give much information that is irrelevant, unbalanced, or erroneous. Take, for example, Cranmer-Byng's theory on the development of poetic meters: "The poetical metres of each age vary according to the requirements of the period. In the beginning we find the short metre of the Odes [i.e., *Book of Songs*] well adapted to the needs of a simpler civilisation. Gradually, as society becomes more complex, the verse needs grow until finally the five and seven-character line of the T'ang dynasty appears, and after that the form has become stereotyped." Such nonsense as this is hardly more fanciful than his translations, which are more correctly effusions inspired by original Chinese poems. "Quiet Night Thoughts" by Li Po (701-762) (in nos. **11,12**) is a poem of twenty words which Cranmer-Byng in *Lute of Jade* has expanded to fifty-four words. Not the only error in his translation is the misreading of "Fatherland" for "old home":

> Athwart the bed
> I watch the moonbeams cast a trail
> So bright, so cold, so frail.
> That for a space it gleams
> Like hoar-frost on the margin of my dreams.

> I raise my head,—
> The splendid moon I see:
> Then droop my head,
> And sink to dreams of thee—
> My Fatherland, of thee!

3. Budd, Charles, tr. *Chinese Poems.* London: Oxford University Press, 1912. 174 pp.

This volume is one of the earliest general anthologies of Chinese poetry in English translation. Western readers unfamiliar with Chinese were acquainted with little besides the *Book of Songs,* and Budd's object in publishing this book was "to correct this false perspective, not by assailing the Shi-King [i.e. *Book of Songs*], but by bringing into view a few of the poets and a few of their poems (which can only be very inadequately set forth in translations by a writer who is not a poet), and thus make a beginning in an undertaking that will be, I hope, continued and perfected by men who have more leisure and greater poetical skill than I possess." Specifically, Budd had in mind the poets of the Han (206 B.C. - A.D. 220), T'ang (618-907), and Sung (960-1279) dynasties, even though he did not translate many Sung poems.

His introduction on the history and construction of Chinese poetry is perhaps less valuable as a treatment of Chinese poetry than as a document illustrating the state of our knowledge of Chinese literature in 1912. There are brief and generally accurate notes on the poets translated, but the book itself does not seem to be organized according to any principle in particular. Budd employed rhyme in his translations as did many early translators, a practice which has since been all but abandoned. Although his translations are fairly accurate, they are incredibly wordy; for example, the following quatrain represents ten words (two lines) of the original:

> I was but fifteen when I left my friends
> For distant climes to fight our Country's foe,
> And now I'm eighty—back for the first time
> To see the home I left so long ago.

It is characteristic of Budd's verse that, in Alexander Pope's words, "ten low words oft creep in one dull line." He is to be congratulated, however, on a freedom from gross error which has marred so many translations since his day.

4. Waley, Arthur, tr. *A Hundred and Seventy Chinese Poems.* New York: Alfred A. Knopf, 1919. 243 pp.
5. ———. *More Translations from the Chinese.* London: George Allen & Unwin, 1919. 109 pp.
6. ———. *The Temple and Other Poems.* New York: Alfred A. Knopf, 1923. 150 pp.
7. ———. *Translations from the Chinese.* Illus. by Cyrus Leroy Baldridge. New York: Alfred A. Knopf, 1941. 325 pp.
8. ———. *Chinese Poems: Selected from "170 Chinese Poems," "More Translations from the Chinese," "The Temple," and "The Book of Songs."* London: George Allen & Unwin, 1946. 213 pp.

These five volumes are the general anthologies of Chinese verse published over the last fifty years by Arthur Waley, surely the most distinguished translator and interpreter of East Asian literature in this century. It was Waley's practice to select only those poems that could readily be translated into English; therefore, his anthologies are not intended to be representative of Chinese poetry as a whole. But his profound scholarship and unfailing ear have produced translations of the greatest accuracy which are at the same time poems in their own right, and these are surely representative of Chinese poetry at its best. In *A Hundred and Seventy Chinese Poems,* he explains his method of translation, a method he perfected over the years: "I have . . .tried to produce regular rhythmic effects similar to those of the original. Each character in the Chinese is represented by a stress in the English; but between the stresses unstressed syllables are of course interposed. . . . I have not used rhyme because it is impossible to produce in English rhyme-effects at all similar to those of the original, where the same rhyme sometimes runs through a whole poem." This earliest volume contains an essay on poetic technique and a historical survey of Chinese poetry. The first part of the volume is made up of Chinese poems from the first century B.C. to the seventeenth century A.D.; the last part of the volume consists of a biographical note on Po Chü-i (772-846) and translations from about sixty of his poems. Waley later wrote a biography of Po Chü-i (no. **61**).

More Translations from the Chinese contains mostly T'ang dynasty (618-907) poems but is again heavily balanced in favor of Po Chü-i, presumably because his poems, being simpler than those of other T'ang poets, are more readily translated into good English verse. *The Temple* includes an excellent study of Chinese poetry prior to the T'ang dynasty and some of the first English translations of *fu* or "rhyme-prose" poetry (see Introduction, pp. 5-6). *Translations from the Chinese* and *Chinese Poems* are indebted to the earlier volumes and contain no new poetry translations, although in *Translations from the Chinese* there are a few T'ang dynasty literary tales. Of these two collections, *Chinese Poems* is preferable; it lists sources of the poem and is more thoroughly annotated, and better indexed than the other volume. *Translations* gives the impression of belonging to the gift book category: it is oversized (7" x 11"), wasteful of space, unindexed, and almost unannotated. Furthermore, the Baldridge illustrations, gaudy and most un-Chinese, are only disconcerting. The translations, however, are still Waley's, and in whatever form they appear, they are still the beginning student's best introduction to Chinese poetry as great poetry.

> **9.** Ayscough, Florence, tr. *Fir-Flower Tablets: Poems Translated from the Chinese.* English versions by Amy Lowell. Boston: Houghton Mifflin Co., 1921. xcv, 227 pp.

Fir-Flower Tablets is one of the best-known collaborative efforts in Chinese poetry translation. The work is important not only because of Amy Lowell's hand in it but also because of the method of translation it employs and the theory about

Chinese characters that underlies it. The authors' intention was to provide poems as close in spirit to the originals as possible; their selection does not intend to be representative. There are about ninety poems by Li Po (701-762), thirteen poems by Tu Fu (712-770), and about twenty-five poems by some twenty other poets from earliest times through the tenth century A.D. The volume closes with nineteen "Written Pictures," mostly from the nineteenth century.

Amy Lowell describes the method of collaboration as follows:

Mrs. Ayscough would first write out the poem in Chinese. Not in the Chinese characters, of course, but in transliteration. Opposite every word she put the various meanings of it which accorded with its place in the text, since I could not use a Chinese dictionary. She also gave the analyses of whatever characters seemed to her to require it. The lines were carefully indicated, and to these lines I have, as a rule, strictly adhered. . . . I had, in fact, four different means of approach to a poem. The Chinese text, for rhyme-scheme and rhythm; the dictionary meanings of the words; the analyses of characters; and, for the fourth, a careful paraphrase by Mrs. Ayscough, to which she added copious notes to acquaint me with all the allusions . . . that she deemed it necessary for me to know.

A number of the poems seem to have been passed back and forth several times before Mrs. Ayscough and Miss Lowell were satisfied with them.

The theory underlying these translations is that all Chinese characters are pictures of the things they represent and that a translator should ideally account for these pictorial representations as well as etymological connotations of all characters in a poem. For example, the first line of a well-known poem by Li Po, "You ask why I stay in the green mountains," is translated as, "He asks why I perch in these green jade hills." Since the word for *green* also means *jade* in some contexts, the word *jade* is introduced into this line, although *jade-green* might have been less misleading. Even though the word *stay* is frequently used of birds, surely to translate it as *perch* is irrelevant—not to say ridiculous—in the context of this poem. The shortcomings of this theory become obvious if one considers what the translation of an English poem into Chinese would be like if the translator attempts to account for American as well as English connotations of every word. Failing, as it does, to give accurate representation of Chinese poetry in English, this volume is nevertheless important and interesting for the experiment it undertook.

10. Ts'ai T'ing-kan, Admiral, tr. *Chinese Poems in English Rhyme*. Chicago: University of Chicago Press, 1932. xxi, 146 pp.

The foreword to this volume claims that it is "the first English translation of Chinese poems by a native of China." If indeed such is the case, then it was an auspicious beginning. Admiral Ts'ai's translations, while usually free, are not misleadingly so, and his rhymed verses are surely some of the more successful ever attempted. This volume is limited to translations of T'ang (618-907) and Sung (960-1279) dynasty poets, about eighty of whom are represented by 122 poems, all four lines in length. The first thirty-nine poems have five words to a line and the rest have seven words to a line. Both the five-and seven-word poems are arranged according to the four seasons. Most poets are represented by only one poem as Admiral Ts'ai's object was to give wide rather than deep sampling; choice was also undoubtedly made according to translatability.

"In translating these poems," writes Admiral Ts'ai, "the rule followed was that each Chinese word be equal to one foot or two syllables in English. Thus, in poems of five Chinese words in each line the pentameter was used. In poems of seven words in a line, the hexameter was generally used. There are a few exceptions to the foregoing rules." His preoccupation with translation into good English rhymed verse is evident from a lengthy discussion of the problem in the preface. The Chinese text accompanies each of his translations, and some fourteen pages of annotation have been relegated to an appendix. There are also an author index and chronological tables. While Ts'ai's translations have none of the wordiness that marks most translations into rhymed verse, they suffer on occasion from unnecessary liberties with the original and often from awkward and disconcerting inversions, e.g., "Those borders wild no bird or blossoms cheer," "For faded flowers beyond my door none seems to care," and "Deep floods of spring each ere to me will come." Translations into rhyme have not generally been successful; Admiral Ts'ai has been considerably more aware of the pitfalls than most of the others, which, of course, is why he has been the better able to avoid them.

11. *Chinese Love Poems From Most Ancient to Modern Times.* Decorations by Paul McPharlen. Mount Vernon, New York: Peter Pauper Press, 1942. 89 pp.
12. *The Jade Flute: Chinese Poems in Prose.* Mount Vernon, New York: Peter Pauper Press, 1960. 61 pp.

These small volumes are representative of those miscellaneous compilations that aim at being not so much books as gifts or, perhaps, elaborate greeting cards. Both volumes, especially the first, are attractively printed, illustrated and bound. *Chinese Love Poems* contains translations from a number of translators of whom Arthur Waley, Teresa Li, Ch'u Ta-kao and Soame Jenyns are particularly worthy of mention. Less reliable, even if no less acceptable as poetry, are the versions by Gertrude Joerissen and Peter Rudolf (Englished versions of French translations by Franz Toursaint and Judith Gautier, respectively); Joerissen and Rudolf are responsible for more than one hundred of the 174 poems in the volume.

Chinese Love Poems must be used with caution; so much cannot be said for *The Jade Flute.* This latter volume, considerably slighter than *Chinese Love Poems*, acknowledges neither editor, illustrator, nor translator. The poets' names are transliterated inconsistently (some are in standard romanization, some are not); it is most consistent, however, in its general style and, above all, in its merciless inaccuracy. We might take as an example what is probably the most famous single Chinese poem, "Quiet Night Thoughts" by Li Po (701-762). A literal translation might look like this:

> The bright moonlight at the foot of my bed
> Made me think there was frost on the ground;
> I raised my head to gaze on the bright (or, mountain) moon,
> Then lowered my head and thought of my old home.

In *The Jade Flute*, this poem has been distorted almost past recognition:

> Look: Moonlight shining on my bed. Or is it the white
> of frost?
>
> Raising my head, I see the moon over mountains. Lowering
> it, I remember all my debts and errors.

Such misrepresentation speaks for itself.

13. Payne, Robert, ed. *The White Pony: An Anthology of Chinese Poetry from the Earliest Times to the Present Day, Newly Translated.* New York: John Day, 1947, 414 pp. (Paperback, New American Library, Mentor Books).

The White Pony, a fairly comprehensive collection of Chinese lyric poetry, begins with a generous sampling of pieces from the *Book of Songs*, the oldest anthology of Chinese poetry, and ends with what is probably Mao Tse-tung's most famous poem, "The Snow." The collection includes an enthusiastic introduction to Chinese poetry and brief comments on most of the poets represented. The most important early Chinese poets—Ch'ü Yüan, T'ao Yüan-ming, Wang Wei, Li Po, Tu Fu, and Po Chü-i—are represented adequately for a collection of such broad scope.

The translators have not adhered to rhyme but have attempted "to translate the poems as simply and literally as possible. . . . The Chinese has therefore been translated line by line." The method of translation, as described by Payne, is as follows: "Chinese scholars were asked to translate the poems they believed they were most fitted to translate on the basis of their experience and scholarship; these were then revised by me and submitted to them, until final agreement was reached." The result is relative accuracy in translation throughout.

Since the majority of poems translated in *The White Pony* represent "regular verse" (*shih*, peoms of generally uniform line length), verse of irregular line length, the important poetry of the last one thousand years, has been slighted.

Minor drawbacks include occasional inaccuracies with respect to historical fact and infelicitous lapses in critical judgment (e.g., Li Po, at one point, is compared to William Blake). Nevertheless, this volume provides the broadest sampling of any collection of Chinese poetry in English and is undoubtedly the best introduction to the subject for the general reader.

14.   Alley, Rewi, tr. *The People Speak Out: Translations of Poems and Songs of the People of China.* Peking: n.p., 1954. x, 107 pp.

15.   ———. *The People Sing: More Translation of Poems and Songs of the People of China.* Peking: n.p., 1958. 446 pp.

A preface to the first of these volumes states, "From the earliest times in China, the chief medium for protest against oppression and social injustice has been the poetic forms and songs in which the people have been able to express themselves." This is an assertion borne out by a study of Chinese poetry more than by this particular volume; with scarcely a dozen exceptions, the poems in this volume are written by poets, real or self-styled, and only about one-fourth of the book contains poems written earlier than the twentieth century.

The much larger sequel is by far the more substantial volume and represents an effort to show social consciousness in the broadest sense in Chinese poetry from earliest times to the present. The first two-thirds of *The People Sing* is a comprehensive if not a particularly representative collection of pre-twentieth-century poetry. Understandably, T'ao Yüan-ming (365-427), Tu Fu (712-770), and Po Chü-i (772-846) are emphasized because of their attraction to the simple life or their concern for common people; but, there are eighteen Sung dynasty (960-1279) poems and thirty-two poems from the Yüan (1279-1368), Ming (1368-1644) and Ch'ing (1644-1911) dynasties as well. The next hundred pages contain poems written between 1920 and 1956 by such poets as Kuo Mo-jo, Wen Yi-to, and Mao Tse-tung. The last part of the volume consists of folk songs. The translator has preferred what he calls "clarity and simplicity": his translations are accurate rather than poetic. The volumes primarily suffer from a rather distorted principle of selection; otherwise, they form a fairly presentable general anthology of Chinese poetry.

16.   Hart, Henry H., tr. *Poems of the Hundred Names: A Short Introduction to the Study of Chinese Poetry with Illustrative Translations.* Stanford: Stanford University Press, 1954. 263 pp.

This anthology contains more than two hundred short lyrics from ancient times through the Ch'ing dynasty (1644-1911). Its chief distinction lies in its attempt at broad representation and in the unprecedented attention it pays to the famous Chinese poetesses, Tzu Yeh (fl. fourth century A.D.) and several others. The short introduction to the study of Chinese poetry is composed of four short essays. "The Spirit of Chinese Poetry" discusses Chinese poetry as the mirror of the thought and spirit of the Chinese and their preoccupations with love, friendship, separation, and nature. "The History of Chinese Poetry" is an outline survey which understandably gives the briefest of treatments to its subject. "The Technique of Chinese Poetry" deals with the formal characteristics of Chinese verse. The most interesting of the brief essays is the last one, which discusses "The Problems of Translation." Hart has given careful thought to this problem and his remarks should prove most illuminating to a beginner. He describes his own method as follows:

The poem is carefully studied in the original. The text is restored to its original form as far as possible. A rough literal translation is then made, the meanings of each word and phrase being noted. After a few readings of this translation, the words and phrases fall into a pattern which, to the translator, appears to convey the proper meaning of the poem. The words and their meanings thus approximate the

Chinese syllables and their connotations, as far as the differences in the two languages permit. The final translation should be in metrical English. The pattern may vary; invariable, however, is fidelity to the original text. [p. 30]

Such an insight is valuable, and it goes far to explain the success of Hart's translations. The volume is further enhanced by a bibliography of Western-language studies and translations —some quite obscure—and of Chinese and Japanese studies and poetry collections.

17. Kwôck, C.H., and McHugh, Vincent, trs. *Why I Live on the Mountain: 30 Chinese Poems from the Great Dynasties.* Paperbound. San Francisco: Golden Mountain Press, 1958. 32 pp.

18. McHugh, Vincent, and Kwôck, C.H., trs. *The Lady and the Hermit: 30 Chinese Poems by Li Ch'ing-chao of the Sung and Wang Fan-chih of the T'ang.* Paperbound. San Francisco: Golden Mountain Press, 1962. 32 pp.

When a poem is highly allusive, a translator must either expand or annotate his English version. Aside from this complication, literal accuracy is by no means beyond reach. What taxes the translator is the problem of re-creating for the English reader the experience of reading the Chinese poem. Chinese poetry invariably rhymes, but rhyme is not its outstanding characteristic. Certainly the best translators have been ready enough to sacrifice it for other gains; translations into rhyme have generally failed, anyway. C.H. Kwôck and Vincent McHugh have been remarkably successful in duplicating the experience of reading poetry in Chinese. Their method is to be as verbally literal as possible, playing down without obscuring the grammatical connections between words. Lines in the original have been broken up into short and somewhat choppy English lines and have been arranged on the page so that the eye must move from phrase to phrase. As a result, while a Kwôck–McHugh translation looks nothing like a Chinese poem, one has the sensation of reading a poem in the original Chinese; the apparently disconnected words and phrases in one of their translations closely resemble the Chinese line with its five or seven independent characters.

Why I Live on the Mountain consists of translations from T'ang (618-907) and Sung (960-1279) poets; the poems of Li Ch'ing-chao and Wang Fan-chih (the lady and the hermit, respectively) are a study in contrast, "Yin and Yang in startling black-and-white."

19.   Rexroth, Kenneth, tr. *One Hundred Poems from the Chinese.* New York: New Directions, 1959. xiv, 160 pp. (Paperback).

This volume is divided into two parts—part one consists of translations of thirty-five poems by Tu Fu (712-770), whose work the translator has known since adolescence; part two consists of translations of nearly eighty poems by Sung dynasty (960-1279) poets, notably Mei Yao-ch'en, Su Tung-p'o, Li Ch'ing-chao, and Lu Yu. Of his translations from Tu Fu, Rexroth writes: "In some cases they are very free, in others as exact as possible, depending on how I felt in relation to the particular poem at the time." He did not at first have the Chinese text to about half of the Sung poems; these he "usually translated from other Western languages, mostly the French of Soulié de Morant and G. Margouliès. Both of these have considerable merit as poetry in their own right. Later I took my translations to the originals and changed them around to suit myself."

His aim has been to produce valid English poems: "I make no claim for the book as a piece of oriental scholarship. Just some poems." In general, it may be said that Rexroth's translations, while consistently pleasing as poetry, are quite free, and on occasion one is tempted to suggest that the translator has actually misread his originals. Furthermore, the poems do not preserve any particular order, and they are sometimes difficult to identify. This is not to find fault with the book for not being what it never set out to be; it is, however, a collection of poems from the Chinese, and simple identification of these poems could hardly be called "oriental scholarship." The beginning student of Chinese poetry should read these poems

only against authoritative versions like those of Hawkes and
Hung for Tu Fu (nos. **55, 60**) and Watson for Su Tung-p'o (no.
66).

20. Ch'en, Jerome, and Bullock, Michael, trs. *Poems of Soli-
   tude*. London: Abelard-Schuman, 1960. 118 pp.

This collection is a substantial sampling of the work of six
Chinese poets who span the eight hundred years from A.D. 200
to about 1000. They have been chosen because they can be
readily translated into English, because they have not been
much translated before, and because they trace the progress of
poetic genres from so-called old-style verse of five words per
line to *tz'u* poetry (poetry of uneven line length).
   Juan Chi (210-263) is represented by fifteen poems from his
sequence, *Poems of My Heart*. These poems are in the form of
five-character ancient-style verse, containing an indefinite num-
ber of five-character lines and rhyming on even-numbered
lines. The other ancient-style verse form, consisting of seven
characters to a line, is illustrated by eighteen poems by Pao
Chao (414-466).
   New-style verse, or regulated verse, for which the T'ang
dynasty (618-907) is noted, is considerably more disciplined
than old-style verse. New-style verse has either five or seven
words to a line, but either four or eight lines to a poem. Fur-
thermore, it demands certain parallel constructions and tonal
patterns that were not demanded in old-style verse. At its
worst, it is a dull exercise in imitation; at its best, it is most
successful. Tu Fu in particular excelled at it. New-style verse is
offered here in "Forty poems of the River Wang" by Wang Wei
(699-759) and his friend P'ai Ti (714-?) and by nine poems of
the late T'ang poet Li Ho (791-817).
   The last of the important traditional verse forms is the *tz'u*.
Tz'u were written to the tunes of pre-existing songs, and the
only rules were those set down by the demands of the indi-
vidual song itself. Line length can vary considerably—some-
times from three to ten words within the same *tz'u*. Thir-
teen poems by Li Yü (937-978) represent this important

contribution of the Sung dynasty (960–1279). A general intro-
duction briefly discusses the poetic genres in question, and
there is a brief essay on each poet. These poems are accurate
and read extremely well; the book itself has an unusually at-
tractive format. *Poems of Solitude* is one of the works in the
UNESCO Chinese Translations Series.

21.   Davis, A.R., ed. *The Penguin Book of Chinese Verse*. Tr. by
Robert Kotewall and Norman L. Smith. Baltimore: Pen-
guin Books, 1962. lxxi, 84 pp. (Paperback).

This volume contains about 175 poems by 128 poets from
earliest times to the present day. For all the poets there are
brief biographical sketches located not very conveniently in
the table of contents together with sources for all the poems.
There are four pages of brief notes and an index of poets at the
back of the volume. The excellent introduction by A.R. Davis
discusses some formal and spiritual characteristics of Chinese
poetry, its themes and its aesthetic qualities. "This anthology
was not compiled with the object of illustrating the history of
poetry in China," Davis writes. "The two translators worked
together over a number of years, translating at their will until
the pages grew. In the end they produced a selection of
Chinese verse, ranging more widely than most which have yet
appeared, over the whole period of verse-writing in China, a
period of more than 2,500 years. They translated what pleased
them and what seemed to go well into English without too
much regard to native Chinese views of poetic stature."
The great majority of selections from T'ang dynasty
(618–907) or earlier are *shih* (poems of uniform line length) of
four or eight lines; they have, however, with twenty-eight
poems, represented *tz'u* poetry very adequately considering
the size of the collection. The volume closes with two or three
translations from modern vernacular poems by Liu Ta-pai, Hu
Shih, and Ping Hsin. These translations by Kotewall and
Smith are uniformly accurate and readable, and while the an-
thology itself does not give a balanced picture of Chinese po-
etry, as a whole it conveys very well the varied temperaments

of the great *shih* and *tz'u* poets and the wide range of subject matter in their poetry.

22.   Birch, Cyril, comp. and ed. *Anthology of Chinese Literature: From Earliest Times to the Fourteenth Century.* New York: Grove Press, 1965. xxxiv, 492 pp. (Paperback, Evergreen Book).

This is the first of two volumes which together form the first comprehensive anthology of Chinese literature from earliest times to the present. (The second volume was published too late for inclusion in this Guide). The excellence of this first volume is only what one might expect from Professor Birch, his associate editor, Professor Donald Keene, and a most distinguished group of contributors—translators of the stature of Arthur Waley, David Hawkes, Burton Watson, to name only three. Approximately one-half of the selections appear in print for the first time, having been commissioned for this anthology; of the other half, however, many were practically inaccessible, having first been published in out-of-the-way periodicals or books long out of print. Obviously no effort has been spared to obtain for this volume the most accurate and the most polished translations.

The Chou dynasty (1122-221 B.C.) is represented by generous selections from the *Book of Songs* and the *Songs of Ch'u.* Four *fu* (rhyme-prose) are included to illustrate that outstanding contribution of the Han dynasty (206 B.C.-A.D. 220), and forty-two poems and Lu Chi's celebrated "Essay on Literature" represent the Period of Division (220-589). The T'ang dynasty (618-907), the golden age of Chinese poetry, is very adequately treated, and from the Sung dynasty (960-1279) there are no less than forty-eight *tz'u* (poems of irregular line length). There is an introductory essay to the volume and each section is prefaced by a brief critical piece that discusses the historical setting of selections translated. The volume concludes with a brief bibliography.

The major drawback of this anthology is that the selections are so little annotated. For the *Book of Songs, Songs of Ch'u,*

"The Shang-lin Park," and, above all, Lu Chi's "Essay on Literature," there is not a single note. These are works which at times are almost hopelessly obscure; a few notes would have helped. The reader of this indispensable anthology should refer to studies like Burton Watson's *Early Chinese Literature* and Liu Wu-chi's *An Introduction to Chinese Literature* (nos. **46, 87**).

23. Liu Shih Shun, tr. *One Hundred and One Chinese Poems.* Hong Kong: Hong Kong University Press, 1967. xxix, 173 pp.

"If one were to set down all the serious mistakes made in English translations of Chinese poetry during the last half century or more," writes Professor Liu, "one would easily fill a fair-sized volume." To demonstrate the need for a more faithful rendering, the translator has limited himself to a few illustrations, with special reference to some of his better-known predecessors. He fills a fair-sized preface with some errors made by English translators from L. Cranmer-Byng to Arthur Waley, giving the impression that he comes forward with a considerably greater grasp of his subject than previous translators have enjoyed. One wishes that he had discussed the problems of translation from Chinese; certainly his strictures on his predecessors' works are not very enlightening and at times they are unjustifiable.

Professor Liu's translation method tends to aim at being literal rather than literary. The volume concentrates on the poetry of the T'ang (618–907) and Sung (960–1279) dynasties and gives examples of both *shih* (poetry of uniform line length) and *tz'u* (poetry of uneven line length). The Chinese text faces each translation; the notes, while kept to a minimum, are adequate. Of the 101 poems translated here, eighty-eight have been attempted before, and these are all listed in a most helpful two-way concordance in the appendix, which also contains a good bibliography and poet-title indices. It is an excellent study-text for a beginning student of Chinese poetry because it enables him to read the Chinese text against reliable translations; the reference to still other translations of poems (in one case as many as thirteen) should give him valuable insights into the art of translation itself.

24. Frodsham, J.D., tr. and annot., and Ch'ing Hsi, collaborator. *An Anthology of Chinese Verse: Han Wei Chin and the Northern and Southern Dynasties.* London: Oxford University Press, 1967. xliii, 198 pp.

This volume is one of a planned series of four that will attempt to be the first balanced Western-language anthology of Chinese verse. Because the T'ang dynasty (618-907) is associated with China's greatest poetry, translators have given it most of their attention. This is regrettable in so far as the other great Chinese lyricists have been all but neglected. This anthology, amply demonstrating the loss, goes a long way towards filling the gap. The poems included were not selected at random or according to their translatability into English, but were carefully chosen from 7000 poems surviving from the fall of Han in 220 through the Sui dynasties (581-618).

The volume contains only lyric poetry and folk songs and ballads; nevertheless, it represents the very best poetry written during the four hundred years prior to the T'ang dynasty. Of the poets from this period, T'ao Ch'ien is the only one who has come to more than passing attention of Western translators, and indeed, there is only a token representation of T'ao Ch'ien in this volume. It does give overdue recognition to poets like Ts'ao Chih, Juan Chi, Hsi K'ang, Hsieh Ling-yün, Hsieh T'iao, and Yü Hsin, to name only a few. The years following the fall of the Han dynasty were among the most turbulent in Chinese history, and these poems on war and the grief war brings, on wandering and separation, and on the transience of life more than adequately reflect their time.

The translations are accurate, smooth, and sometimes startlingly successful. There is a long introduction to the poetry of the period, there are introductions to the individual poets, and the translations are generously annotated. Chinese literary studies can only benefit greatly from this volume and the three that are promised.

Pre-T'ang Poetry

GENERAL COLLECTIONS

25. *Shih ching. The She King.* (1871). Vol. 4 in *The Chinese Classics.* Tr. by James Legge. Reprinted with minor corrections and added concordance. Hong Kong: Hong Kong University Press, 1960. xii, 785 pp.

26. ————. *The Book of Songs.* Tr. by Arthur Waley. (1937). Paperbound. New York: Grove Press, Evergreen Book, 1960. 349 pp.

27. ————. *The Book of Odes.* Tr. by Bernhard Karlgren. Stockholm: Museum of Far Eastern Antiquities, 1950. 270 pp.

28. ————. *The Confucian Odes: The Classic Anthology as Defined by Confucius.* Tr. by Ezra Pound. Cambridge: Harvard University Press, 1954. xvi, 224 pp. (Paperback, New Directions).

29. Han Ying. *Han Shih Wai Chuan: Han Ying's Illustrations of the Didactic Application of the "Classic of Songs."* Tr. by James R. Hightower. Cambridge: Harvard University Press, 1952. vii, 368 pp.

30. Dembo, L.S. *The Confucian Odes of Ezra Pound: A Critical Appraisal.* Berkeley: University of California Press, 1963. 111 pp.

The *Book of Songs* (*Shih ching*), the oldest collection of Chinese poetry, has been translated a number of times into English. At least four of these translations are, for different reasons, worth studying. The earliest of these translations by James Legge contains a substantial introduction on the origin of the *Shih ching*, its prosody, and its use by the Chinese. There is also a long chapter on Chinese life at the time the *Shih ching* was written. The Legge text includes the poems in the original Chinese, fairly literal (rather than literary) translations, and extremely full notes based, in large part, on the work of traditional Chinese scholars. Along with the copious notes explaining allusions, glossing obscurities and offering alternative translations, the student should profit from those notes that deal with traditional interpretation of the poems. Legge does not often agree with the frequently outlandish interpretations of these charming folk songs, but he surely gives a generous sampling of them. Legge's version is the best one for the beginning student of Chinese who wishes to approach the *Shih ching* in the original, as well as for the student who, although he knows no Chinese, would like to get as close as possible to the Chinese understanding of this great work.

The text of the *Shih ching*, as it has come down to us, divides the 305 poems into three main categories which may be translated as folk songs, court songs, and sacrificial songs. Since some of the poems in each group do not always fit their description, there is considerable controversy over just how the poems were originally arranged. Whatever principle of arrangement the first editors followed, it would seem not to be of great value to the student reading the poems in translation, and Arthur Waley has abandoned the traditional arrangement in favor of an arrangement according to subject matter. The disadvantages (for example, overlapping of subjects) are really minimal, and there is a finding list at the back that will enable one readily to locate any given poem in the original text. Waley's translations are not only accurate; they also attempt to convey some of the charm of the original poems. He has included an introduction on how to appreciate the *Shih ching*, and his translations are frequently interspersed with notes to facilitate understanding of the individual poems.

Bernhard Karlgren's version, entitled *The Book of Odes*, contains the original Chinese text, as does Legge's, and a translation far more literal than either Legge's or Waley's. Karlgren follows the traditional arrangement of the poems and has numbered them consecutively from 1 to 305. The translation is accurate (indeed, Waley acknowledges his indebtedness to Karlgren in the revised *Book of Songs*) and may safely be considered a standard against which to measure other versions. Its unique feature is its transliteration of the entire text. Karlgren has been the most important Western student of ancient

Chinese pronunciation, and the transliteration of the *Odes* includes his conjectures on how many of the words were pronounced in remote antiquity.

The most recent English version of the *Shih ching* was translated by Ezra Pound, one of the foremost poets of the twentieth century. His version, while not exactly a translation, is by no means the least successful artistic representation of the ancient collection. The frequent use of archaic English and Latin and Greek headings tend to confer upon Pound's version some semblance of the antiquity for which the *Shih ching* has been so long revered by the Chinese. Pound has not always understood the texts, but he has not failed to react sensitively to the poems themselves and to provide shrewd insights into the quality of the poetry. His *Confucian Odes* is one of those rare translations that becomes a classic in its own right and should not be overlooked by any student of Chinese poetry. It should, however, be eventually studied against the original or a translation like Karlgren's. Indeed, such an approach would enhance one's appreciation for both the original and the translation. L.S. Dembo's study is an enlightening appreciation of Pound's work, but it is not entirely sound in its remarks about the *Shih ching* itself, Mr. Dembo being a critic rather than a sinologist. Its importance is as a study of the influence of a Chinese classic on a foremost modern poet.

It is generally agreed that the *Shih ching* is mostly a collection of folk songs, gathered from many parts of China. Confucius was very fond of these songs, many of them probably old even in his day, and encouraged the study of them. Exactly what value (other than literary) he saw in them is not really clear, since his remarks about them in the *Analects* are suggestive rather than specific. When the *Shih ching* took its place as one of the official Confucian Classics, it seems to have been assumed among Confucianists that their master would never have advocated the study of a mere collection of lovely folk songs; clearly, Confucius saw in them much more than meets the eye. Accordingly, it was the lifework of many scholars to write expositions and commentaries on the *Shih ching*, placing special emphasis on its moral or ethical content. Fortunately, there is a complete English version of one of these commentaries, the *Han shih wai chuan,* translated by Professor James R. Hightower. It is not a systematic commentary, and indeed the short anecdotes that constitute the work may be read independently. Quite aside from being an entertaining collection of anecdotes, the *Han shih wai chuan* is the best source for studying the traditional Chinese understanding of their greatest classic.

31. *Ch'u Tz'u. Li Sao and Other Poems of Chu Yuan.* Tr. by Yang Hsien-yi and Gladys Yang. Peking: Foreign Languages Press, 1955. xvii, 97 pp.

32. ———. *Ch'u Tz'u: The Songs of the South, An Ancient Chinese Anthology.* Tr. by David Hawkes. Oxford: Oxford University Press, 1959. x,229 pp. (Paperback, Beacon Press).

33. Waley, Arthur. *The Nine Songs: A Study of Shamanism in Ancient China.* London: George Allen & Unwin, 1955. 64 pp.

The *Ch'u Tz'u,* or *Songs of Ch'u,* is the second great collection of Chinese poetry and comes down to us from the second century A.D. when it reached its final form. Most of the poems in the collection, however, have traditionally been attributed to Ch'ü Yüan (fl. fourth century B.C.), the first Chinese poet whose name is known to us. Modern scholars, like Professor Hawkes, have been cautious about attributing these poems to Ch'ü Yüan, but Ch'ü Yüan is regarded by critics from the People's Republic as not only the probable author of most of the poems but also as one of the first great Chinese patriots.

Kuo Mo-jo's "Sketch of Chu Yuan," which introduces the Yang translations of *Li Sao and Other Poems,* provides a good example of this hero worship, although it should not be the sole basis on which the Yang translation is judged. In an attempt to approximate the meter of the original, the Yangs have employed what would seem to be the least appropriate English verse form: the closed couplet, hardly a proper vehicle for Ch'ü Yüan's luxuriant and impassioned "Li Sao." Nevertheless, the translated verses are fairly creditable and pleasing. With one exception, the Yangs have not provided notes for their translations, choosing rather to sacrifice literal accuracy in the interest of making the poems as self-explanatory as possible; as a result, their translation is eminently readable and a good introduction to the *Ch'u Tz'u*.

The Hawkes translation is accurate rather than literary. It is a complete translation of the *Ch'u Tz'u* anthology with an excellent introduction to its prosody and origins and it includes a translation of the official biography of Ch'ü Yüan. There are brief critical introductions to each poem as well, and the text is generously annotated throughout.

Arthur Waley, in his *Nine Songs*, a translation and study of one of the important works in the *Ch'u Tz'u*, traces the origin of these poems (actually eleven rather than nine in number) to the shamanistic or spirit-intermediary religious practices of ancient China. His introduction deals with this shaman tradition in some detail and then presents the thesis that the "Nine Songs" were originally "a set of rites in honour of the principal deities of the land of Ch'u." Running commentaries accompany each poem.

INDIVIDUAL POETS

34.   Hughes, E.R. *Two Chinese Poets: Vignettes of Han Life and Thought*. Princeton: Princeton University Press, 1960. xv, 266 pp.

As the title suggests, this book is concerned primarily with social and cultural aspects of Han times as reflected in the writings of two Chinese poets. The two poets are Pan Ku (A.D. 32-92) and Chang Heng (A.D. 78-139), each of whom wrote *fu* poems on the Western and the Eastern Capitals, Ch'ang-an and Loyang, respectively. Chang Heng's two poems were written about a generation later than Pan Ku's, and it was Professor Hughes's intention to study the contrast between the two periods as reflected in the poems. His primary interest is not in the literary aspects of their two pairs of *fu* poems; in fact, he does not hesitate to summarize when direct translation would not serve his purpose. Nevertheless, he has made quite faithful, if partial, translations of four difficult poems and has written extensive and highly illuminating commentaries dealing with them mostly as a primary historical source on the life and thought of Han times (ca. 100 B.C.–A.D. 100).

35.   Ts'ai Wen-chi. *The Eighteen Laments.* Tr. by Rewi Alley. Peking: World Press, 1963. 43 pp.

The Eighteen Laments is a translation of a series of eighteen lyric-narrative poems attributed to Ts'ai Yen or Ts'ai Wen-chi, to use her courtesy name. Although her authorship of the poems has been frequently contested by scholars, *The Eighteen Laments* do describe an experience that Ts'ai Wen-chi actually underwent during the last years of the second century.

According to the official life of Ts'ai Wen-chi in *The History of the Latter Han Dynasty,* it was about 195, during the confusion of the breakup of the Han Dynasty, that she was led away captive by the Hu barbarians. During her exile, which lasted for twelve years, she was given in marriage to a barbarian chieftain and gave birth to two sons. Through the intercession of Ts'ao Ts'ao, the famous Chinese general, she was released and brought back to China, where she was remarried to Tung Szu. *The Eighteen Laments* describe, in eighteen stages, her experiences and feelings during her twelve years away from China. They tell of her initial capture, marriage, and separation from home; her longing for familiar faces, customs, food, and language; her loneliness, wandering, cries to Heaven; and her grief at having to leave her children after twelve years.

The poems have been smoothly translated into free verse, and the volume is beautifully illustrated with eighteen parts of an anonymous Ming Dynasty painting of Ts'ai Wen-chi's captivity.

36.   Hsi K'ang. *Hsi K'ang and His Poetical Essay on the Lute.* Tr. and annot. by R.H. Van Gulik. New ed., rev. Tokyo: Sophia University; Tokyo: Peter Brogan, The Voyagers' Press, 1969. 133 pp.

Hsi K'ang (223-262) was one of a group of seven unconventional scholar-artists who are known as the Seven Sages of the Bamboo Grove. This group included, among others, Hsiang Hsiu, the celebrated commentator on Chuang Tzu, and Juan Chi, the poet who is, with the possible exception of Hsi K'ang, best known to posterity from among the members of this coterie.

It is Hsi K'ang's special distinction that he was an eminent lute player: his reputation as a lutanist in China is comparable to Paganini's reputation as a violinist in Italy. Hsi K'ang was unfortunate enough to fall out of favor with powerful men and he was executed together with a friend. Biographical writings all record how, during his last hours, he called for his lute and played. He is surely best known for his long verse essay or *fu* on the lute. In this poem, Hsi K'ang describes the growth of catalpa trees from whose wood lutes are made, the manufacture of lutes, the special beauties of lute music, and the several merits of the lute as an instrument.

Dr. Gulik has written a long introduction to his heavily annotated translation which provides the reader with the historical, philosophical, and literary background necessary to an understanding of the poem. It is unfortunate that all translations of such difficult works as Hsi K'ang's *Lute* are not so completely equipped with material essential to their intelligibility.

37. Lu Chi. *Essay on Literature Written by the Third-Century Chinese Poet Lu Chi.* Tr. by Chen Shih-hsiang. Portland, Maine: Anthoensen Press, 1953. xxxv pp. (Reprinted by Grove Press in *Anthology of Chinese Literature*, ed. by Cyril Birch).

38. ———. *The Art of Letters: Lu Chi's "Wen Fu,"* A.D. 302. Tr. and annot. by E.R. Hughes. Bollingen Series, vol. 29. New York: Pantheon Books, 1951. xviii, 261 pp.

39. ———. *"Rhymeprose on Literature: The Wen-Fu of Lu Chi (A.D. 261-303)."* Tr. and annot. by Achilles Fang. In *Harvard Journal of Asiatic Studies*, vol. 14. (1951). pp. 527-566. (Reprinted by Harvard University Press in *Studies in Chinese Literature*, ed. by J.L. Bishop).

40. Knoerle, Sister Mary Gregory. "The Poetic Theories of Lu Chi, with a Brief Comparison with Horace's *Ars Poetica*," *Journal of Aesthetics and Art Criticism* 25 (1966): 137–143.

The *Wen Fu* (Essay on Literature) is one of the earliest Chinese works on literary criticism. Like Horace's *Ars Poetica* and Pope's *Essay on Criticism*, the *Wen Fu* is written in verse. The verse form employed is that of the extremely difficult *fu* (see pp. 5–6), which is characterized by rhyme, interspersed prose passages, and intricate verbal parallelism in paired lines. Lu Chi discusses the process of literary composition from the time the writer is inspired until the time he brings his intelligence to bear upon his work; then, he studies the ideal qualities of the different literary genres and how literary works may fail or how they may succeed. This work is extremely difficult to read even with considerable annotation, and it is at times so vague as to drive even the most attentive reader almost to despair.

The three translations listed here differ considerably in the amount of annotation they provide: the Hughes book is primarily a study of the poem, while the Ch'en translation as reprinted in *Anthology of Chinese Literature* (no. **22**) is unhappily without any notes. It is suggested that two or three versions be read together. In fact, it is always true that two or three good translations—especially of a difficult work like the *Wen Fu* by Lu Chi—are of immeasurably greater value to the student than is a single translation. In an appendix to the Hughes book, there is a convenient translation of "A Discussion about Literature" by Ts'ao P'ei (187–226), one of the first Chinese literary critics.

Mary Gregory Knoerle's essay is a discussion of Lu Chi's notion of what makes a good poem, surely an excellent first approach to a most difficult and often confusing work. Her comparison of Lu Chi with Horace helps to highlight the peculiar characteristics of the Chinese critic against the more familiar Western background of the Roman critic. This essay is recommended because it is a nontechnical but sensible treatment of Lu Chi and his theories; the beginning student can find no better introduction to the *Wen Fu*.

41.   T'ao Ch'ien. *T'ao the Hermit: Sixty Poems by T'ao Chien (365-427)*. Tr., intro., and annot. by William Acker. London: Thames and Hudson, 1952. 157 pp.

42.   ————. *The Poems of T'ao Ch'ien*. Tr. by Lily Pao-Hu Chang and Marjorie Sinclair. Honolulu: University of Hawaii Press, 1953. ix, 133 pp.

Of all Chinese poets, perhaps T'ao Ch'ien (or T'ao Yüanming) is the one most readily apprehended by the Western reader. Not only does he write in a comparatively simple language that has invited frequent translation, but he also writes about subjects that are familiar and attractive to humanity at large. T'ao Ch'ien lived in an age when existence was extremely perilous, especially for those who, like himself, were in government service. He was naturally inclined toward the simple life in the country in companionship with a few intimate friends, and it was his great pleasure to escape from stultifying official life.

These two translations of T'ao Ch'ien's verse complement one another admirably. While short of being a complete translation, *T'ao the Hermit* contains a long introduction on T'ao's life and poetry. Furthermore, it has considerably more annotations than the Chang-Sinclair volume. The latter has the virtue of being complete and contains, in addition to the poetry translations, a nearly contemporary biographical sketch of the poet. Both translations are accurate, and the student should profit from the comparison of two reliable versions of the same poems.

43.   Liu Hsieh. *The Literary Mind and the Carving of Dragons*. Tr. and annot. by Vincent Yu-chung Shih. New York: Columbia University Press, 1959. xlvi, 298 pp.

The Literary Mind and the Carving of Dragons has been the most influential work of traditional Chinese literary criticism.

Its author, Liu Hsieh, flourished during the first part of the sixth century A.D., and his work is the crowning achievement of some three centuries of literary criticism. Professor Shih has written a long introduction on literary criticism in China up to Liu's time and beyond.

The Literary Mind itself consists of a preface and forty-nine sections, the first twenty-five of which discuss, in turn and usually by pairs, the genres that Liu Hsieh understood as being literary rather than merely practical in nature. He not only describes the ideal nature of these several genres, but gives brief histories of them with special attention to some of their greatest practitioners. The last twenty-four sections deal with literary technique and excellence, and they amount almost to a poet's *vade mecum* with its advice on how to write and how not to write. Shih's completely dependable translation is provided with numerous notes that greatly assist in the understanding of a most valuable but difficult work.

BIOGRAPHICAL AND CRITICAL WORKS

44. Ssu-ma Ch'ien. "The Biographies of Ch'ü Yüan and Master Chia." In *Records of the Grand Historian of China,* tr. by Burton Watson. 2 vols. Vol. 1, pp. 499–516. New York: Columbia University Press, 1961.

The lives and works of Ch'ü Yüan and Chia I are similar enough justifiably to be considered together in *Records of the Grand Historian* even though they lived more than one hundred years apart: Ch'ü Yüan in the fourth and third centuries B.C. and Chia I in the third. Ch'ü Yüan is sometimes called the father of Chinese poetry (nos. **31, 32**). Like many other Chinese poets, he was also a government official, and although he is remembered for his unwavering loyalty to his sovereign, he was slandered by jealous enemies and fell out of favor at court and lost his position. This unjust punishment accounts for the melancholy pervading his greatest poem, "Li Sao," which means "encountering sorrow." The biography contains a translation of "Embracing the Sands," supposedly written just before Ch'ü Yüan committed suicide.

Chia I was another poet-official who was slandered by his enemies and fell out of favor with his sovereign. Furthermore, he acknowledged Ch'ü Yüan as his master in the art of poetry, and his "Lament for Ch'ü Yüan," included in the biography, is more than a little reminiscent of the earlier poet's work. This life of Chia I includes another long poem, "The Owl," which has sometimes been compared to Edgar Allen Poe's "The Raven." *The Records of the Grand Historian,* which comes down to us from the second century B.C., is very ably translated and annotated by Professor Watson.

45. Ssu-ma Ch'ien. "The Biography of Ssu-ma Hsiang-ju." In *Records of the Grand Historian of China,* tr. by Burton Watson. 2 vols. Vol. 2, pp. 297–342. New York: Columbia University Press, 1961.

Ssu-ma Hsiang-ju (179–117 B.C.) is perhaps the most important poet of the Former Han dynasty (206 B.C.–A.D. 24). He is particularly remembered as the greatest writer of *fu* poetry—a literary form, partly verse and partly prose, which has been infrequently translated into English because of its dazzling but obscure and sometimes archaic language. One of the distinctions of Ssu-ma Hsiang-ju's biography is the inclusion of some of his best-known poems, and Professor Watson has rendered all of them into unusually smooth and accurate English; "Sir Fantasy," "Shang-lin Park," and "The Mighty One" are some of the most important.

Ssu-ma Hsiang-ju is even better remembered by generations of Chinese for his love affair with Cho Wen-chün and their elopement and marriage. Wen-chün's father disowned her, but later relented and gave her a handsome dowry rather than let their poverty bring shame upon himself. Ssu-ma Hsiang-ju's obvious genius won him imperial favor and he held the post of palace attendant for most of his life.

46. Watson, Burton. *Early Chinese Literature.* New York: Columbia University Press, 1962. 304 pp. (Paperback).

Early Chinese Literature is a general introduction to Chinese literature from earliest times to about A.D. 100. Its three sections treat the three main divisions of Chinese literature in the broadest sense: history, philosophy and poetry. The nearly one-hundred-page chapter on ancient Chinese poetry is further divided into four parts: "The *Shih Ching* or *Book of Odes*," "The *Ch'u Tz'u* or *Elegies of Ch'u*," "The Han Fu," and "Songs and Ballads." The section on the *Book of Odes* discusses the division of the book, the verse forms, the language of the *Odes*, and its traditional and modern interpretation. The many excerpts from the *Odes* make this section a highly selective anthology with extremely helpful commentary.

The *Elegies of Ch'u*, no less than the *Odes*, are sometimes extremely obscure and, even in the most attractive translation, seem somewhat forbidding to the reader coming to them for the first time. Again, Professor Watson's commentary, particularly on "Li Sao," the longest poem in the collection, gives the beginner excellent assistance.

The most impressive section is perhaps the one dealing with *fu* of the Han dynasty (206 B.C.-A.D. 220). The *fu*, which may be translated "rhyme-prose," is a long descriptive poem often in dazzling and obscure language which has caused the form, at least as it was produced during the great Han prosperity, to be seldom translated into English. It is to Watson's credit that he has translated the larger part of one of the longest and most difficult of these, Ssu-ma Hsiang-ju's "*Fu* on the Shang-lin Park."

The last section on songs and ballads discusses the folk songs and shorter lyric poetry of the Han dynasty. Judicious in its selection of material for discussion, clearly and informatively written, and, like Watson's other works, reliable in its scholarship, *Early Chinese Literature* is the best introduction to its subject available.

T'ang Poetry

GENERAL COLLECTIONS

47. *T'ang-shih san-pai shou. The Jade Mountain: A Chinese Anthology, Being Three Hundred Poems of the T'ang Dynasty, 618-906.* Tr. by Witter Bynner and Kiang Kang-hu. New York: Alfred A. Knopf, 1929. xxxvii, 300 pp. (Paperback, Doubleday, Anchor Books).

48. ———. *Selections from the Three Hundred Poems of the T'ang Dynasty.* Tr. by Soame Jenyns. Wisdom of the East Series. London: John Murray, 1940. 116 pp. (Paperback, Paragon Book Reprint Corp.).

49. ———. *Further Selection from the Three Hundred Poems of the T'ang Dynasty.* Tr. by Soame Jenyns. Wisdom of the East Series. London: John Murray, 1944. 95 pp. (Paperback, Paragon Book Reprint Corp.).

The *T'ang-shih san-pai shou* or *Three Hundred T'ang Poems* is a collection of poetry put together in the eighteenth century by an anonymous editor. The number *300* (actually, 311) corresponds to the number of poems originally in the Confucian *Book of Songs* (nos. **25-27**), and it also conforms to the saying, "By reading thoroughly three hundred T'ang poems, one will write verse without learning." Although not all of the very finest T'ang dynasty poems are included in this anthology, it has been the best-known and most often read collection since its compilation more than two hundred years ago. The English collection to which it most nearly corresponds is *The Golden Treasury*.

The Jade Mountain is superior in most respects to the two Jenyns volumes: it is a complete translation of the anthology while Jenyns provides only a partial translation. In addition, Witter Bynner collaborated with a Chinese scholar who not only worked with him on the translations but also wrote a most illuminating introduction on Chinese poetry in general and poetry of the T'ang dynasty in particular. They took minor

liberties with the original poems in the interest of more imme-
diate clarity and stylistic smoothness; the translations are gen-
erally of a high literary quality. Appendices provide historical
and geographical information as well as generous notes to the
poems themselves. The Jenyns translations are fully annotated,
but they are not usually elegant. Furthermore, Jenyns arbi-
trarily arranges by subject matter in the first volume and by
author in the second volume, while Bynner and Kiang arrange
by author throughout. As always, the student will profit from
comparison of two translations.

50. Graham, A.C., tr. and intro. *Poems of the Late T'ang.*
Paperbound. Baltimore: Penguin Books, 1965. 175 pp.

The poetry of the early part of the T'ang dynasty (eighth
century) has been translated into English almost since transla-
tion from Chinese poetry began, and Western readers have
long had access to the works of Li Po, Tu Fu, Po Chü-i and
many of their contemporaries—if only, at times, in middling
translations. Certain poets of the ninth century, however, have
been neglected, and A.C. Graham's book is an attempt to fill
this serious gap. It is not, indeed, surprising that the late T'ang
poets have not frequently been rendered. Graham writes,
"During these three centuries obstacles to the translator
steadily multiply—increasing density of language, an allusive-
ness which often forces him to bury a poem in commentary,
elaborate versification which shakes his confidence that the
sacrifice of form for content is necessarily a sound bargain."
Nevertheless, it is precisely because the poetry of this age "ex-
plores the Chinese language to the limit of its resources" that
it should be made available to Western readers; an unaccus-
tomed side of Chinese poetry is seen in the somber melan-
choly of Li Ho and the allusive ambiguity of Li Shang-yin, to
mention only two of the seven poets represented.

There are critical introductions to the individual poets and
an excellent general introduction on the problems of transla-
tion and Graham's solutions to those problems. *Poems of the*

Late T'ang was accepted in the UNESCO Chinese Translations Series.

51.   Waley, Arthur, tr. *Ballads and Stories from Tun-huang.* London: George Allen & Unwin; New York: Macmillan Co., 1960. 273 pp.

In the early part of this century, a Buddhist monk discovered a whole library of manuscripts in a cave at Tun-huang in northwestern China. Many of these found their way to the British Museum and to the Bibliotheque Nationale before some ten thousand were taken to Peking. Even then, some six hundred manuscripts were obtained by a Japanese mission. Many of these manuscripts have little literary interest in themselves, but a few of them provide us with much of the knowledge we have concerning the popular literature of the T'ang dynasty (618-907).

It is from those on popular literature that Arthur Waley selected pieces for inclusion in this volume. Most of the items are prose, but there are several that are either wholly or substantially in narrative verse. The most interesting form is that which alternates prose and verse (*pien-wen*) and which, as recited by professional storytellers, seems to have been a highly popular entertainment in the T'ang dynasty. An afterword to Waley's book gives a fascinating account of the discovery and undercover sale of these very valuable documents. He discusses their literary form and some untranslated pieces in an appendix. The translations themselves are accompanied by explanatory notes, most of which are addressed to the general reader.

INDIVIDUAL POETS

52.   Wang Wei. *Poems by Wang Wei.* Tr. by Chang Yin-nan and Lewis C. Walmsley. Rutland, Vermont: Charles E. Tuttle Co., 1958. 159 pp.

This collection contains more than 160 poems (136 titles) of this early T'ang painter-poet of whom a later poet, Su Tung-p'o, said "there is painting in his poetry and poetry in his painting." This picturesque quality is nowhere more evident than in the poems of four five-character lines, of which about fifty are translated in this volume. Chinese critics have frequently remarked on Wang Wei's ability to paint an entire landscape in a single line.

The translations are divided in the Chinese manner according to poetic types (number of lines and number of words per line) and are prefaced by a brief biography and essays. Annotation has been kept to a minimum, but the poems read well and are generally accurate, allowing for a few minor liberties in translation. Ten paintings are included, either to illustrate Wang Wei's style or "to illustrate the mood of a poem." The untenable and long-discredited notion that the translator must strive to convey all the complexities of every word in the original is evident in the introduction to this book, but it seems not to have materially influenced the translations themselves.

53.   Li Po. *The Works of Li Po: The Chinese Poet.* Tr. by Obata Shigeyoshi. (1922). New York: Paragon Book Reprint Co., 1966. xviii, 236 pp.

The title, *The Works of Li Po,* is somewhat misleading since only about ten percent of Li Po's poems are included; nevertheless, it is, after nearly fifty years, still the only book-length collection of translations from the most famous Chinese poet. Mr. Obata, a Japanese student of Chinese literature, has translated 124 poems by Li Po, 8 poems about Li Po (particularly by his friend Tu Fu), and 3 biographical sketches of Li Po. In addition, he has written a biographical introduction and a bibliography which, though now out of date, lists the more important Li Po items in Western language up through about 1921 and previous translations of poems he has included in his book. The original Chinese texts are found in an appendix.

Obata explains his method of translating in a preface:

A literal translation would often leave a Chinese poem unintelligible unless supplied with a great amount of exegesis, and I did not wish to empty all the rich content of the original into footnotes. I have amplified or paraphrased on many occasions. I have omitted unimportant words here and there. I have discarded, or translated, a number of proper names because, some way or other, Chinese syllables refuse to sing in company with English words.

The result is a collection of poems in very readable English that are allowed to speak for themselves, assisted only by such notes as are necessary for the clarification of a poem. Such notes explain an allusion, provide some bit of background information, or give assistance in interpretation. *The Works of Li Po* may well be recommended as an adequate and representative sampling of Li Po's best and most often read poetry.

54.   Tu Fu. *Tu Fu: Selected Poems.* Comp. by Feng Chih and tr. by Rewi Alley. Peking: Foreign Languages Press, 1962. x, 178 pp.

This volume, published in commemoration of the 1250th birthday of Tu Fu, contains translations of 140 of his poems. It is illustrated with a portrait of Tu Fu, facsimile pages from two early editions of Tu Fu's poetry, and six modern paintings (reproduced in black and white) which were "inspired by the poems."

In his introduction, Feng Chih tells how Tu Fu "sang praises of the people's honesty and fortitude, while exposing and condemning the ruling class for their dissipation and extravagance." Critical literature from Peking is more than a little tinged with socialist bias, and the reader is advised to recognize this fact; for all of Feng Chih's gratitude for Tu Fu's "positive and progressive" political viewpoint, the truth is that the poet was a humanitarian, and as such was sensitive to human suffering including, incidentally, his own.

These translations are scantily annotated, and minor liberties with the original seem to have been taken largely in the interest of simplification. The selection of poems seems fairly representative. It ought to be said, however, that Chinese translations from the People's Republic in general should be used with some caution since the translators are prone to bend or twist the lines in order to make them conform to their beliefs. Such a practice may speak volumes for the translators themselves, but it considerably reduces the value of the translation.

55. Hawkes, David. *A Little Primer of Tu Fu*. Oxford: At the Clarendon Press, 1967. xii, 243 pp.

A Little Primer of Tu Fu contains the thirty-five poems by Tu Fu that are included in the *Three Hundred T'ang Poems* (nos. 47-49), the most famous anthology of Chinese poetry. For each of these poems, the original Chinese text is accompanied by a line-by-line transliteration into *Pin-yin*, the official Chinese transliteration system. There follows a discussion of the title and subject of the poem and a section that studies its form, including such matters as poetic type and rhyme scheme. Next, an exegesis provides a judicious word-by-word literal translation interspersed with notes explaining allusions and problems of usage. Finally, there is a slightly expanded prose translation, which, as the author states in a brief introduction, is intended as a crib rather than as a polished English version. At the back of the volume a section on vocabulary glosses all words and compounds and notes their occurrences in the body of the text.

Professor Hawkes intended this book for people who have little or no knowledge of Chinese. Indeed, it would seem to lend itself admirably to the uses of such students. The volume is completely self-contained, and the student who has worked through it certainly should have "learned something about the Chinese language, something about Chinese poetry, and something about the poet Tu Fu." This is surely the book, among several on Chinese poetry, that brings its reader closest to its subject, and one would hope to see more books like it in the near future.

56. Han-shan. *Cold Mountain: 100 Poems by the T'ang Poet Han-shan*. Tr. and intro. by Burton Watson. (1962). New York and London: Columbia University Press, 1970. 118 pp. (Paperback).

"There is an enormous body of Buddhist poetry in Chinese," writes Professor Watson in his instructive introduction to the present volume, "but it is for the most part no more than rhymed sermonizing, seldom rising above doggerel; for all its doctrinal importance, its literary value has been customarily rated—and rightly so, I think—rather low." As he points out, there are some "doggerel sermons" in the work of the Buddhist poet Han-shan as well, but that Han-shan wrote some admirable verse is borne out clearly by this fine volume of translations.

Most of the poems are eight lines in length and are descriptive of the poet's surroundings, introspective and, at times, shrewdly observant of human nature. Watson does not copy the traditional orthodox Buddhist reading of the poems with its tendency to force, when all else fails, doctrinal soundness. Rather, his less subtle reading lets us see Han-shan, not as the enlightened bodhisattva, but as a man on a kind of spiritual pilgrimage.

The little information available on Han-shan does not include his birth and death dates, but Watson, following modern scholarly opinion, places him in the late eighth and early ninth centuries. As will be clear to anyone who reads these poems, however, the essential Han-shan is revealed in his verse. Not often have poets given so full an account of themselves.

BIOGRAPHICAL AND CRITICAL WORKS

57. Bishop, John L. "Prosodic Elements in T'ang Poetry." In *Indiana University Conference on Oriental-Western Literary Relations*, ed. by Horst Frenz and G.L. Anderson, pp. 49–63. Chapel Hill: University of North Carolina, 1955.

This brief essay, addressed as it is to the general reader, gives a very good idea of "how through verse forms, prosodic details, and poetic devices, a Chinese poem achieves its effects." It begins with a description of the Chinese language, with special emphasis on the four tones. An example of tonal patterns in a Chinese poem illustrates the tonal balance which gives Chinese poetry a musical quality. Bishop is primarily interested in "regulated verse" which conforms to a number of prosodic specifications, and he closes his essay with extended consideration of two T'ang poems, one an eight-line "regulated verse" and the other a four-line "stop short regulated verse." The accompanying transliteration, tone pattern, "Pidgin-English" version and, finally, polished translation also illustrate the process of translation from Chinese into English.

58. Frankel, Hans H., tr. and annot. *Biographies of Meng Hao-jan.* Berkeley and and Los Angeles: University of California Press, 1961, 28 pp.

This is the first of a projected series of translations from official Chinese histories. Meng Hao-jan (691-740) was one of the most important T'ang poets (for translations from his work, see nos. **47-49**), and this pamphlet provides two of the most important sources for information about his life: the biographies in the two official histories of the T'ang dynasty, compiled in the tenth and eleventh centuries, respectively. The first is only a brief notice that tells little more than that he was a poet who failed the civil service examination and held only one official position. The second biography is much fuller, but Meng Hao-jan's poetry is scarcely mentioned. Both biographies gain in clarity from the notes, which occupy more than half the volume. This translation is not designed primarily for the general reader, but it is mentioned here because it is one of the few reliable translations of a Chinese poet's official biography.

59. Waley, Arthur. *The Poetry and Career of Li Po, 701-762* A.D. London: George Allen & Unwin; New York: Macmillan Co., 1950. 123 pp.

The Poetry and Career of Li Po, a biographical essay rather than a full-scale biography, is an excellent account of the life of the Chinese poet best-known to Western readers. Li Po is remembered perhaps as much for his generally unconventional and irresponsible life as for his poetry: he loved wine and was frequently inebriated, he "ran his sword through quite a number of people," and had several wives. Waley also discusses Li Po's knowledge of alchemy, his interest in Taoism, and his fruitless attempts to secure some kind of official post; for contrary to the demands of his own best interests, Li Po inexplicably had never sat for the imperial examinations, the one real avenue to the status and economic security that he seems to have sought for much of his life.

Arthur Waley's study of Li Po provides considerable historical background. Li Po's friends are introduced, along with his patrons and literary executors, the men who held public office during Li Po's lifetime, and the events which they helped to shape. This historical and cultural information is particularly helpful in understanding Li Po's many occasional poems, several of which are translated in Waley's text.

Waley was no admirer of Li Po's life, and the greatest criticism against his book is in the fact that more attention is given to Li Po's personal failings than to the merits of his verse. In fact, an editorial note to the "General Introduction", not supplied by Waley, implies that the book's *raison d'etre* is to preach temperance, if not abstinence, using Li Po as a negative example.

Waley's scholarship is extremely cautious, and he writes with considerable charm, but it is disappointing that he leaves out such Li Po folklore as the legend that he drowned while trying to catch hold of the moon's reflection in the water. The story, almost certainly spurious, may be as close to the spirit of Li Po's best poetry as any fact of his life. The best introduction to Li Po is necessarily his poetry (see especially nos. **47-49, 53**).

60. Hung, William. *Tu Fu: China's Greatest Poet.* Cambridge: Harvard University Press, 1952. x,300 pp.

Although Tu Fu (712-770) may not be quite as well known to Western readers as his famous fellow poet and friend Li Po, not many Chinese would dispute the title conferred on Tu Fu by Professor Hung in the subtitle. English readers are fortunate to have a full-scale biography of Tu Fu, especially as it is the best in any language, including Chinese. In a preface to this volume, Professor Hung talks about his lifelong study of Tu Fu which began when he was only thirteen. While his enthusiasm and obvious love for his subject never wane, he never succumbs to uncritical hero worship, an inherent danger in an undertaking of this kind. The book's value as a biography is further enhanced by 374 translations of Tu Fu's poems. Rather than "worry over form," Professor Hung has translated into prose in an attempt "to convey only Tu Fu's thought and spirit."

In the introduction, he discusses at some length the problems both of the biographer and of the translator of Tu Fu and provides the reader with a brief sketch of Tu Fu's biographers, Chinese and Western, and a most helpful survey of his Western translators. Particularly instructive is his critique on the Ayscough-Lowell method of translation (see no. 9) which tries to take into account the etymologies of every word in the original. The grain of truth on which that method is based has helped to account for its wide influence, but Professor Hung explains quite clearly why it is untenable. This book carries us along the course of Tu Fu's career and allows us to see his poetry take shape under the press of daily life. Nowhere better than here, perhaps, can we study the intimate relationship between poetry and life.

61. Waley, Arthur. *The Life and Times of Po Chü-i, 772–846* A.D. London: George Allen & Unwin, 1949. 238 pp.

Maurice Collis, one of the first reviewers of this biography, wrote that "it will provide the general reader to whom it is addressed with a clear and exact notion of China when it was the most civilized place in the world. Nowhere else can so much information be obtained about life in the T'ang dynasty." It is this encyclopedic quality of Waley's book that is most impressive. Po Chü-i, the best-known poet of the second half of the T'ang dynasty, was also a government official. (It might be more accurate to say that he was a poet when time permitted.) He was, during most of his life, to some extent involved with the political and historical events of the age. Waley allows us to see Po Chü-i against the background of the age in all its cultural and political complexity.

Po Chü-i felt strongly that poetry had a decided ethical function; the poems that he prized the most were the satirical ballads, many of which dealt movingly with the suffering of the common people under an irresponsible regime. In contrast to other poets, Po Chü-i's poetry is more easily translated into English because he made such an effort to be understood even by the uneducated. Few poets have been so widely read: one ninth-century writer tells about a street laborer whose body was tattooed with lines from Po's poetry.

Waley's biography contains complete or partial translations of some one hundred poems, most of which supply information about Po's life. Elsewhere (see annotations of *Translations from the Chinese* and *Chinese Poems*, nos. **7, 8**) he has translated about a hundred other poems which, since they are dated, may very conveniently be read with this biography.

Post-T'ang Poetry

62. Candlin, Clara M., tr. *The Herald Wind: Translations of Sung Dynasty Poems, Lyrics and Songs.* Intro. by L. Cranmer-Byng and foreword by Dr. Hu Shih. London: John Murray, 1933. 113 pp. (Paperback, Paragon Book Reprint Corp.).

Until the publication of *The Herald Wind*, translations from Chinese poetry were almost exclusively translations of poems of the *shih* type (poems of uniform line length), both because there are many more specimens of *shih* than there are of any other poetic type and because *shih* poems are in many ways less difficult to translate than are other forms. Conspicuously absent were translations of *tz'u* poetry (poetry of uneven line length), perhaps the most considerable new literary direction of the Sung dynasty (960–1279).

Candlin's book is still the most important collection of *tz'u* in English. About sixty of the eighty poems translated are of the *tz'u* type, mostly from the Sung dynasty, although she has included poets of the T'ang (618–907) and Yüan (1279–1368) dynasties as well. Notably, there are four poems apiece by Huang T'ing-chien (1045–1105) and Chou Pang-yen (1057–1121), six poems by Lu Yu (1125–1201), and nine poems by Hsin Ch'i-chi (1140–1207).

An introductory essay by L. Cranmer-Byng deals more or less with the poetry of the Sung and a brief note describes the characteristics of *tz'u* poetry and its later development. There are very brief introductions to the individual poets, but no notes. Lines of verse in the original poems have usually been broken into two or more lines in the translation, which often results in unnecessary choppiness. The translations themselves are somewhat free but generally accurate.

63. Yang, Richard F.S., and Metzger, Charles R., trs. *Fifty Songs of the Yüan: Poetry of the Thirteenth Century China.*

With introduction, appendices and notes. London: George Allen & Unwin, 1967. 151 pp.

The fifty songs, or *ch'ü*, translated in the present volume are examples of the poetic form that was dominant during the Yüan dynasty (1279–1368). Composed to conform to an already existing tune, the *ch'ü* was a development of the earlier *tz'u* of the Sung dynasty, which it closely resembles. The versatile *ch'ü* was also composed in sets which functioned in the Yüan drama as arias.

In a brief introductory background sketch, Yang and Metzger describe their method of translation:

We have chosen to hold as faithfully as possible to syllable count, to imagery, to tone, and to the sense of each poem since we consider these indispensable to the proper translation of *ch'ü*. Faithfulness to rhyme-scheme appears to us unrewardingly awkward, given the different natures of the English and Chinese languages. [p. 7]

The main body of the volume consists of Chinese texts and translations of the fifty poems, but its value is greatly enhanced by the appendices, which include appropriate discussions of Chinese pronunciation and Chinese characters and, most important, transliterations, literal translations, and "first draft" translations of each poem along with a few explanatory notes. The translators have thus given the reader an insight into the problems of translating a most difficult form of Chinese poetry. Taken together, the three English versions are most illuminating and give a good idea of the content of the original poems; however, the final versions by themselves seem needlessly obscure. This is a result of the translators' complete faithfulness to line length in the original. They have sometimes had to sacrifice content to line length, and it appears that greater clarity would have resulted from a slightly more flexible scheme. Nevertheless, the volume is an excellent introduction to *ch'ü* poetry either for the student of poetics or for the student of Chinese literature.

64. Hsü Kai-yu, tr. and ed. *Twentieth Century Chinese Poetry: An Anthology.* Garden City: Doubleday and Co., 1963. xliv, 434 pp. (Paperback, Cornell University Press).

This volume contains translations of more than four hundred poems by forty-four poets whose works have appeared since about 1920. Professor Hsu does not present the poets in strict chronological order (most of the poems are, however, dated); he has chosen rather to present them as they are associated with one of five schools or groups: the Pioneers, the Crescent School, the Metaphysical Poets, the Symbolists, and the Independents (and others). Of these groups, perhaps only the Crescent was a self-styled literary school, but the headings are nevertheless useful, both because they are widely used and because they single out the most important contributions to the development of twentieth-century Chinese poetry.

A long introduction contrasts modern with traditional Chinese poetry and discusses each of the groups of poets in turn. There are introductions to each poet varying from one to ten pages in length depending upon the poet's importance or complexity. These introductions include critical appreciation as well as biographical information. One of the great strengths of this anthology lies in Hsu's knowledge of Western poetry, which has enabled him to perceive and discuss Western influences on modern Chinese poets. This book is the most comprehensive and best-informed study of its kind and is recommended without reservation to the student approaching modern Chinese poetry for the first time.

65. All-China Federation of Democratic Youth, comp. *Songs of New China.* Peking: Foreign Languages Press, 1953. 47 pp.

Poetry and music have been intimately connected since the *Book of Songs,* some of which must date from about 1000 B.C. Even though several of the songs are not necessarily recent, the present volume may be taken as representative of the poet-musician's art as it has flourished since the establishment of the People's Republic of China in 1949. Here are fourteen songs, complete in most cases with piano accompaniment. Lyrics are both in Chinese characters and in romanization; English translations have been relegated to an appendix.

Songs of New China cannot be said to exhibit much variety in subject matter, all but one of the songs being patriotic. They are all written in the colloquial language, and so they do not resist translation. Plainly, they do not survive it either. The artistry (such as it is) and content of these songs may be illustrated with this rousing first verse of "Songs in Praise of Mao Tse-tung":

> You have made our land a lovely garden, Mao Tse-tung,
> You are the inspiration of our life, Mao Tse-tung,
> We know you have our welfare at heart, Mao Tse-tung,
> You are the saviour of our people, Mao Tse-tung,
> O hail Mao Tse-tung,
> Long live Mao Tse-tung!
> Hurrah! Hurrah! Hurrah! Hurrah! Hurrah! H-u-r-r-a-h!

Another example is from the song "Cotton-Spinning":

> A basket clasped firmly with both our hands
> Off to town we are with the cotton yarn.
> The yarn goes to the co-operative store,
> The co-operative is like a home to us all.
> Spin...and spin...and spin...and spin,
> In the village every home spins its own cotton.

Perhaps it will not readily be believed, but the music to which these songs are written noticeably diminishes their appeal.

INDIVIDUAL POETS

66. Su Tung-p'o. *Su Tung-p'o: Selections from a Sung Dynasty Poet.* Tr. and intro. by Burton Watson. New York: Columbia University Press, 1965. x, 139 pp.

This volume contains translations of eighty-three poems by Su Tung-p'o (1037-1101), the greatest poet of the Sung dynasty (960-1279). Su Tung-p'o's complete works represent most of the traditional Chinese literary genres (he was, indeed, one of the great prose masters). Professor Watson's collection represents three of the most important poetic forms: the *shih* (poetry of uniform line length), the *tz'u* (poetry of uneven line length, which was one of the outstanding achievements of Su's age), and the *fu* (prose poem). The latter form is illustrated by excellent translations of the "Two Prose Poems on the Red Cliff."

Watson is a humble as well as an excellent translator, and he graciously acknowledges a debt to Tamaki Ogawa, whose Japanese translations of Su Tung-p'o "provided the foundation" for his own. These translations are presented in chronological order (each one is dated) and can very conveniently be read along with Lin Yutang's excellent biography of Su (no. **75**). An introduction to the volume gives an outline of Su's life and helpful background information on the poetic genres represented. The poems themselves are generously but judiciously annotated throughout. This volume was accepted in the UNESCO Chinese translations series.

67. Lu Yu. *The Rapier of Lu: Patriot Poet of China*. Tr. with biography by Clara M. Candlin. London: John Murray, 1946. 68 pp.

This collection contains some forty poems by Lu Yu (1125-1210), the patriotic poet of the Southern Sung dynasty (1129-1279). It was during this turbulent period that Tartar invaders slowly took over China from the north. The dynasty they finally founded in 1279, the Yüan dynasty, lasted until 1368. Lu Yu is remembered for his spirited outcry against the barbarian encroachments and his grief for his country's plight.

The Rapier of Lu, published as it was soon after World War II, has a patriotic emphasis ("Modern China sees in these far-off events of history a parallel with their country's present plight, and for this reason Lu Yu's stirring words are on the lips of China's patriotic youth to-day"). It does not, however, ignore Lu Yu's other poetry, and most of the poems are grouped under "Travel" or "Nature." Even these poems, though, with their deep melancholy remind us of Lu Yu's concern for his homeland. The volume includes a biographical introduction and a brief chronology of Lu Yu's life and times. Although some may find disconcernting the translator's habit of chopping lines from the original into two short lines in English, the translations themselves, while somewhat free, are generally accurate.

68. Wimsatt, Genevieve, tr. "The Tale of Meng Chiang: A 'Drum Story' in Five Cantos." In *The Wisdom of China and India*, ed. by Lin Yutang. pp. 909-931. New York: The Modern Library, 1955.

The story of Meng Chiang Nü (Lady Meng Chiang) is set in the infamous Ch'in dynasty (221-206 B.C.), when so many men were conscripted by order of Shih Huang, the so-called First Emperor, to build the Great Wall. Fan Ch'i-liang, Meng Chiang's husband, is sent as a laborer to the far northeast, and his wife begins to worry that he, a frail scholar, will be inadequately clothed during the bitter winter. So perilous is the journey that none can be persuaded to carry a parcel of clothing to Fan, so she undertakes the trip herself. Most of the tale is concerned with this difficult journey and her gradual loss of health and beauty. After traveling summer and autumn, she arrives at the Great Wall in time to meet two of her husband's friends who have buried him in the Wall and are on their way to perform rites for him. She is taken to the place where he is buried, and when she cries out for him the Wall bursts open. Clasping his bones she throws herself into the sea.

Many forms of this story exist: short story, drama and, as in the present instance, narrative poetry. Drum stories are recited to the accompaniment of a hand-drum. This poetic version probably dates from about the middle of the eighteenth century and is written in rhymed couplets with seven words to a line. The Wimsatt translation is free but reasonably accurate and is, for the most part, in appropriately rhythmical rhymed couplets.

69. Kuo Mo-jo. *Selected Poems from the Goddesses.* Tr. by John Lester and A.C. Barnes. Peking: Foreign Languages Press, 1958. 67 pp.

This volume contains thirty-four poems from a collection that was first published in 1921. In a brief preface to the second edition, Kuo Mo-jo seems almost reluctant to see these poems in print again after so many years and asks that they "be taken as recordings of the age in which they are written." Kuo Mo-jo has had a most varied career, as can be seen from a short biographical notice appended to this volume. He has written plays, literary criticism, and studies of ancient China as well as poetry.

This volume of verse should give Western readers a good idea of the kind of experimentation carried out by early twentieth-century Chinese poets in their search for a poetic, particularly with respect to their use of Western models. Kuo Mo-jo shows familiarity with Goethe, Whitman, Byron, and Shelley, to name four obvious influences, but his poems are still very much a Chinese product: he is no servile imitator. This poetry is, however, highly self-conscious, sometimes painfully aware that it is a not-very-sure-footed venture into strange territory. Preoccupied as it is with the theme of rebirth or resurrection, somehow his poetry does not seem to get itself born. It is poetry in a Western manner, and in English it seems even more imitative than it actually is; in China in the early 1920s, it was a bold venture indeed. This poetry deserves to be read today, if only as a recording of the age in which it was written.

70. Mao Tse-tung. *Nineteen Poems.* Tr. by Andrew Boyd and Gladys Yang. Peking: Foreign Languages Press, 1958. 62 pp.

Tsang K'eh-chia, in the preface writes: "Himself a lover and a master of classical Chinese poetry, Mao Tse-tung is not restricted by traditional forms, or fettered by old rules. In his hands these rigid patterns become thoroughly flexible—they appear a medium as free and unhampering as water." What he says ten lines further on is perhaps closer to the truth: "The translation of poetry is a most difficult task. This is especially true of classical Chinese poetry with its definite forms, fixed number of characters to each line, and the clearly specified rhyming schemes and patterns of long and short tones." The truth is that Mao Tse-tung has not written in the modern style at all. His poems are in the traditional style, in this case the *tz'u* style (in which the number of words to a line and tone pattern depend upon the tune to which the poem is written), which flourished during the Sung dynasty (960-1279). Chairman Mao seems himself to feel somewhat awkward about having written poems in the traditional manner rather than in the freer modern manner. Mao's protestations to the contrary, however, his achievement in *Nineteen Poems* is by no means contemptible. Mao's best poems are permeated with patriotic fervor, but, happily, they manage to avoid socialist jargon.

BIOGRAPHICAL AND CRITICAL WORKS

71.   Yoshikawa Kōjirō. *An Introduction to Sung Poetry*. Tr. by Burton Watson. Cambridge: Harvard University Press, 1967. xiii, 191 pp.

There is a tendency to associate each age in Chinese history with a particular and characteristic genre that was produced or enjoyed its height of creativity during that age. Thus it is that the T'ang dynasty (618-907) has been acknowledged as the golden age of *shih* poetry (poetry of five or seven words to a line; see introduction p. 6) and the Sung dynasty (906-1279) as the great age of *tz'u* poetry (songs of uneven line length; see introduction p. 12). One unfortunate result of this kind of admittedly convenient pigeon-holing is that the *shih* poetry of the Sung dynasty has been often neglected, even by Chinese scholars who have given almost all their attention to the *tz'u*.

Professor Yoshikawa differs radically in his viewpoint:

The rise and spread of the *tz'u* form, because it represented a new development in the history of Chinese poetry, has been regarded as of great importance by recent literary historians. It is probable that they have in fact attached too much importance to the form which, as a rule, was used almost exclusively to express minor states of emotion. As in the past, the main stream of poetic literature continued to employ the *shih* form, and the most important expressions of feeling were entrusted to this form rather than to the *tz'u*.

In a long first chapter, Professor Yoshikawa considers the nature of Sung poetry, its content and diction, and contrasts it with T'ang poetry. The rest of the book is devoted to a history of *shih* poetry during the Sung dynasty which includes a discussion of works by about twenty of the more outstanding poets and several minor poets as well. About 150 poems are quoted as illustrations. This study, in Professor Watson's readable translation, goes a great way toward filling another of those many gaps in our knowledge of Chinese literature which one fears would otherwise have been long neglected.

72. Hsiao Ch'ien. *Etching of a Tormented Age.* London: George Allen & Unwin, 1942. 48 pp.

This brief essay is a good introduction to twentieth-century Chinese literature. Scarcely six pages are devoted to poetry, but in those six pages Hsiao discusses early twentieth-century reaction to traditional poetry, directions taken by the new poets, the place of vernacular poetry in modern Chinese literature as a whole, and Western influences on the new poetry. There are some almost spectacularly successful examples of modern Chinese drama and fiction; the short stories, novels, and plays of Lu Hsün, Mao Tun, Lao She, and Ts'ao Yü show these writers to be worthy of a high position in world literature. Modern Chinese poetry, however, has not been as prosperous, and Hsiao is well aware, not only of its shortcomings, but also of its inherent disadvantages, breaking, as it does, with a three-thousand year history of traditional poetry. Brief and informal, *Etching of a Tormented Age* is nevertheless a handy survey.

73. Ting Yi. *A Short History of Modern Chinese Literature.* Tr. by Chang Hsing-lien and others. Peking: Foreign Languages Press, 1959. 310 pp.

Unfortunately, this book is the only study that attempts to treat all of modern Chinese literature—fiction, drama, and poetry—since 1919, the year that saw the beginning of the modern educational and linguistic reform known as the May Fourth Movement. The task is by no means an easy one, and if it is ever accomplished by a Western scholar, it will have to take into account the vast body of diverse studies that are available on every aspect of twentieth-century Chinese culture. Ting Yi has not seen fit to put himself to any such inconvenience. His role is twofold: as a historian, he has arranged his material in roughly chronological order with a certain amount of factual information, notably dates (births, deaths, publications) and names (writers and literary societies); as a literary critic, he has acquitted himself admirably, if one is to accept his socialist view that criticism should either glorify or roundly damn. His remarks on one of the early literary schools, the Crescent Society, may be taken as representative: "In the very first issue of their monthly *Crescent* in 1928, they made clear their hostile attitude towards revolutionary literature. In the introductory remarks in this issue entitled 'The Attitude of the Crescent,' they stated their opposition to thirteen kinds of writers, among whom were 'the utilitarians,' 'attackers,' 'extremists,' 'pedlars,' 'sloganeers,' '*ism*-ists,' and the 'hotheaded.' Their target was revolutionary literature." Ting Yi is an attacker, an extremist, a sloganeer, and a hotheaded *ism*-ist. As such, he provides us with an excellent example of socialist literary criticism. It is, indeed, as such an example that his *Short History* has its greatest value.

74. Liu, James T.C. *Ou-Yang Hsiu: An Eleventh-Century Neo-Confucianist.* Stanford: Stanford University Press, 1967. xii, 220 pp.

In a prologue to this work, Professor Liu writes: "One has the urge to climb a mountain, as the saying goes, simply because it is there. The desire to study a great man is similar: he cannot be ignored. And as climbing a mountain gives a grander view of the country surrounding it, so studying a key historical figure gives us a finer perspective of his whole era. These are our interests in Ou-yang Hsiu." Ou-yang Hsiu (1007–1072) is one of those figures whose varied career touched so many facets of his time that a study of him must give one a particularly full exposure to the age in which he lived. Ou-yang Hsiu is, to be sure, mainly remembered as one of the foremost poets of the Northern Sung period (960–1126), but Professor Liu is concerned with Ou-yang's times and with his many-sided career as well.

The first half of the book deals with his life and times and the last half is concerned with Ou-yang as classicist, historian, political theorist and philosopher. If the twelve or fifteen pages that are devoted to his poetry seem too meager, they should also remind us that most Chinese poets have had occupations and interests other than poetry. Certainly, Ou-yang Hsiu's accomplishments and influence have been most outstanding, and they are very fully and ably treated in Liu's book.

75. Lin Yutang. *The Gay Genius: The Life and Times of Su Tungpo.* (1947). Connecticut: Greenwood Press, 1971. xii, 370 pp.

One of the first full-length biographies of a Chinese poet, *The Gay Genius* is also one of the most ample. Lin Yutang early in his book mentions the wealth of material pertinent to Su Tung-p'o's life, and much of the material is described in an eleven-page appendix to the volume. There is no way to summarize Lin's book. It is an especially leisurely, reflective biography; some will think it marred by the author's frequent homespun digressions. While this is not a fictionalized biography, Lin has used his skill as a novelist to bring characters and places to life with vivid descriptions. So clearly has he seen into the heart of his subject that the reader cannot help but come to understand Su Tung-p'o and to acquire an appreciation for his writings.

Su Tung-p'o (1036-1101) was a poet and essayist of the first rank, the most illustrious of the famous Su family scholars (who included Su Tung-p'o, his father and his brother). While recognized by some of the finest minds of the day such as Ou-yang Hsiu (see no. **74**), Su was hated by a faction of influential courtiers whose pettiness contrasts sharply with Su's greatness. He was sent into exile on outrageous charges but managed to do some of his greatest work in comparative poverty. Some will disagree with Lin Yutang's harsh treatment of Wang An-shih (1021-1086), the reformer whose means Su Tung-p'o so deplored: modern historians have tended not to hold him personally responsible for the economically calamitous results of his refoms.

One might wish that Lin had used standard transliterations of Chinese names: his simplified system is a great inconvenience to one not acquainted with Su's life and times.

76. Waley, Arthur. *Yüan Mei: Eighteenth Century Chinese Poet.* Stanford: Stanford University Press, 1956. 227 pp. (Paperback).

Yüan Mei (1716-1797) was one of the most celebrated poets of the Ch'ing dynasty (1644-1911). Extremely precocious, he became a member of the board of scholars known as the Han-lin academy by the age of twenty-three. For nearly ten years afterwards, he held the office of prefect, notably in Nanking, where he found life hectic. In 1749, he resigned from his post and bought an estate which was called the *Sui Yüan* ("Sui Garden"), later to be his sobriquet. During the next years, we follow his writing, his association with friends, his concubines, the scandals in his private life that were always ready to erupt, and his yearly bouts with malaria.

In addition to his poetry and his miscellaneous writing, for which he later came to be paid handsomely, he wrote a volume of random *Jottings* (*Sui Pi*) and a collection of supernatural stories entitled *What Confucius Never Spoke Of* (i.e., ghosts and spirits). This collection, perhaps more generally known to Westerners than his poetry, is represented very generously in

Waley's study. Near the end of his life, he published a volume of *Poetry Talks* which contains poems, poems with anecdotes, stories about poets, and autobiographical fragments. His last work was a *Cookery Book*, which was published in 1797.

Arthur Waley has presented Yüan Mei against the background of his age, giving a vivid picture of a man of letters of the Ch'ing dynasty—his friends, activities, and preoccupations. One of the great successes of this book is the lively English translation from his prose works and his correspondences; Yüan Mei's poetry is represented by translations from almost one hundred poems.

General References

77. Giles, Herbert A. *A History of Chinese Literature.* (1901). New York: Grove Press, 1958. 448 pp. (Paperback, Evergreen Book).
78. Lee Shao-chang. "Chinese Literature." In *Encyclopedia of Literature,* comp. by Joseph T. Shipley. Vol. 1, pp. 143-165. New York: Philosophical Library, 1946.
79. Hightower, James Robert. *Topics in Chinese Literature.* Paperbound. Cambridge: Harvard University Press, 1950. ix, 141 pp.
80. Davis, A.R. "Chinese Literature." In *Literatures of the East,* ed. by Eric B. Ceadel. pp. 131-160. London: John Murray, 1953; New York: Grove Press, 1959.
81. Wang Chi-chen. "Chinese Poetry." In *Dictionary of World Literature,* comp. by Joseph T. Shipley. (1953). pp. 52-54. New Jersey: Littlefield, Adams & Co., 1960.
82. Feng Yüan-chün. *A Short History of Classical Chinese Literature.* Tr. by Yang Hsien-yi and Gladys Yang. Peking: Foreign Languages Press, 1958. 132 pp.
83. Ch'en Shou-yi. *Chinese Literature: A Historical Introduction.* New York: Ronald Press, 1961. xii, 665 pp.
84. Kaltenmark, Odile. *Chinese Literature.* Tr. from the French by Anne-Marie Geoghegan. New York: Walker & Co., 1964. 146 pp.
85. Lai Ming. *A History of Chinese Literature.* New York: John Day Co., 1964. xv, 439 pp. (Paperback, Capricorn Books).
86. Bishop, John L., and Baxter, Glen W. "Chinese Poetry." In *Encyclopedia of Poetry and Poetics,* ed. by Alex Preminger. pp. 117-124. Princeton: Princeton University Press, 1965.
87. Liu Wu-chi. *An Introduction to Chinese Literature.* Bloomington: Indiana University Press, 1966. xii, 321 pp.

These eleven works, listed above by original date of publication, may conveniently be classified under three headings:

studies of Chinese literary genres, outline histories of Chinese literature, and full-length histories of Chinese literature. Of the three studies of Chinese literary genres, Professor Hightower's *Topics* is the more comprehensive, covering, as it does, prose as well as poetry. It is the purpose of this authoritative study to "provide students with some of the factual data on which an historical survey of Chinese literature may be based." The book is arranged roughly by chronology and so deals with each important literary genre as it comes to prominence in the history of Chinese literature. Professor Hightower defines each genre and then traces its significant developments in later periods of Chinese history. To each of the essays is appended a bibliography that lists studies and translations of the genre under consideration. Hightower's book is the only one of its kind and has long been considered a standard reference tool.

The other genre study, Professor Wang's "Chinese Poetry," is much shorter than Hightower's and is restricted to a consideration of the poetic types. It discusses briefly but cogently the four principal genres of Chinese poetry: *shih, fu, tz'u,* and *ch'ü.* The essay by Professors Bishop and Baxter is an authoritative and readable treatment of the language of Chinese poetry, its history, style, and content. Less hurried than the Wang article, it mentions some of the more important poets and poems and includes a generous reading list at the end.

Of the four outlines of Chinese literature, Professor Lee's is perhaps the least formal. It pays attention to history and prosody, but it is much more an enthusiastic appreciation than a critical survey. Furthermore, it is somewhat unbalanced in its treatment (Confucius gets twelve lines; Lin Yutang gets ten), and it does not observe standard romanization practices. A.R. Davis has a keener awareness of the essential, and his brief essay may be taken as a preface to the generous and careful bibliography he provides. Lee's and Davis's outlines together form an extremely useful syllabus for one who wants to familiarize himself with Chinese literature and some of its representative works.

Feng Yüan-chün's *Short History* has, as might be expected, a strong political bias and is not above occasional distortion. The critical resources open to her are severely limited so that she sees Chinese literature as one long protest against unenlightened tyranny and oppression. Since the socialist critics have read social consciousness back into authors who are established by almost universal consent, Miss Feng generally avoids imbalance in her treatment or selection.

The usefulness of Kaltenmark's *Chinese Literature* is perhaps limited by the fact that he combines extreme brevity with the broadest possible definition of Chinese literature and tries to deal with topics such as history, philosophy, and scholarship. As a result, there is less information on poetry than is to be found in much shorter works such as those by Bishop and Baxter or even Davis. It is a fairly competent factual outline, which would be more helpful if it contained a reading list.

Herbert A. Giles's *History of Chinese Literature* purports to be the "first attempt made in any language, including Chinese, to produce a history of Chinese literature." It is now considerably out of date, especially in its treatment of drama and fiction; it is probably most reliable in its treatment of early poetry, although it perpetuates such errors as the notion that Wang Wei was a physician and that Ssu-ma Hsiang-ju's poems "have not survived." Its generally sound critical appraisals are supported by considerable sampling from the original Chinese—almost always in Giles's rhymed English verse.

Professor Ch'en's *Chinese Literature* is the fullest treatment of Chinese literature in English. It was obviously written over a long period of time however, and the almost inevitable inconsistencies were not rectified by careful editing. Some parts of the book may be a bit confusing, but it does contain a large number of translations, has drawn heavily from some of the best Chinese scholarship (although sometimes out of date and unacknowledged), and is particularly strong in its treatment of the historical background of Chinese literature. It would have benefited from notes and a bibliography.

Lai Ming's *A History of Chinese Literature* takes a more traditional approach in what might be called its "golden age" theory of Chinese literature, which sees each age as having produced one or two characteristic genres. It concerns itself completely with the most outstanding writers and works and it quotes so fully that it is more like an anthology than a history. It does not use standard romanization and so it is liable to be confusing if not used with care.

Professor Liu Wu-chi's *Introduction to Chinese Literature* does not present itself as a comprehensive history of its subject: Professor Liu is well aware of what such a task would involve. It is a survey of some of the most important developments in Chinese literary history. The author's intentions are to "give the non-specialist some idea of the continuous progress and lasting splendor of Chinese literature, of its vast corpus and high attainments." So remarkable is his success that one does not know what to praise first: the breadth of his scholarship, the perfect soundness of his critical judgment, or the beauty and clarity of his prose style. Fully annotated, this book also contains a selected bibliography, a chronological chart of Chinese literature, and a glossary of Chinese words. It is without doubt the one study that is essential for the student who is looking for a reliable and judicious guide to Chinese literature.

88. Fenollosa, Ernest. *The Chinese Written Character as a Medium for Poetry.* Ed. by Ezra Pound. (1936). San Francisco: City Lights Books, 1968. 45 pp.

This brief essay has had an influence far out of proportion to its length. Ernest Fenollosa, who is remembered for his studies on Chinese and Japanese art, left a draft of his essay, and after his death in 1908, it came, along with his other notes on Chinese poetry, into the hands of Ezra Pound. It is well known that Pound's earliest English versions of Chinese poems were based on Fenollosa's notes; Pound's own knowledge of Chinese was, at least at first, limited to Fenollosa's essay, *The Chinese Written Character.* As editor of the essay, Pound did "little more than remove a few repetitions and shape a few sentences."

Fenollosa's thesis is that every Chinese character has built into it its etymology; English words have lost their heritage and so are considerably handicapped as media for poetry. Somehow, as we read English words, we are not made aware of their origins and backgrounds, but as we read a page in Chinese the experience is enriched by the wealth of association found in each character. Furthermore, in Fenollosa's view, the translator must convey some of this multiplicity of meaning if he is to approach fair representation of the original.

The fact is that Chinese words must be understood in terms of context, and context always greatly restricts the number of possible meanings. Etymological considerations, especially Fenollosa's own quasi-etymological fantasies, are not frequently relevant to the meaning of a word in a line of Chinese poetry. Although Fenollosa's essay has influenced modern poets in England and America, it will only confuse the beginning student of Chinese language and poetry.

89. Davidson, Martha. *A List of Published Translations from Chinese into English, French, and German.* Part 1: Literature, Exclusive of Poetry; Part 2: Poetry. Washington, D.C.: American Council of Learned Societies, 1957. xxx, 462 pp.

Part I of this standard reference work lists translations of fiction and drama from their beginnings through the early twentieth century; Part II lists translations of poetry, essays, and miscellaneous prose from Ch'ü Yüan (343-290 B.C.) through the Sung dynasty (960-1279). Part II, on poetry, is arranged according to dynasties and, within dynasties, in alphabetical order of the poets' surnames. This reference work is extremely valuable because translations of Chinese works have been so widely scattered in numerous and unexpected volumes and journals. In its attempt to be comprehensive, this work lists all pieces that claim Chinese origin; it is not and could not be annotated and so is not intended as a guide to accurate translations.

90. Liu, James J.Y. *The Art of Chinese Poetry.* Chicago: University of Chicago Press, 1962. xvi, 166 pp.

This study, divided into three parts, is directed toward "the English-speaking reader who has acquired some knowledge of and taste for Chinese poetry through translation." "The Chinese Language as a Medium of Poetic Expression" discusses the structure and meaning of Chinese characters; sound, tone and versification; and style and content of Chinese poetry. The second section, "Some Traditional Chinese Views of Poetry," treats four important ways in which the function of poetry has been understood in China—as didacticism, as a means of self-expression, as a literary exercise, and as contemplation. In showing the development of these not-always-mutually-exclusive views of poetry, Professor Liu quotes generously from Chinese poets and critics. The third section of the book, "Towards a Synthesis," considers the four traditional views of poetry critically to "see if it is possible to effect a synthesis among them, with modifications and additional ideas." Having arrived at the view that poetry is an exploration of different worlds of experience and of the resources of languages, Liu proceeds to considerations of imagery and symbolism; allusions, quotations, and borrowing; and, finally, antithesis in Chinese poetry.

The Art of Chinese Poetry, while not a book for the beginner, is nontechnical in its approach and unique in providing remarkably full equipment for a good critical study of Chinese poetry. It is one of the few indispensable works in English.

INTRODUCTION: DRAMA

In China, as in other countries, there is evidence that some kind of dramatic art existed during the earliest periods that can be reconstructed by the historians. Certainly Chinese drama is indebted to religious ceremony for much of its early development, and the shamanistic rites, with their dances, songs, and impersonation had much about them that were dramatic. The so-called "hundred entertainments" of the Han dynasty—the jugglers, singers, dancers, acrobats and storytellers—made considerable contributions to the development of drama which, as A.C. Scott has pointed out, is "a synthesis of music, dance, song and speech which are absolutely interrelated and dependent on each other."

The drama in the mature form in which we know it today seems to have begun to come into its own during the T'ang dynasty (618-907). The famous Emperor Ming of the T'ang became the most celebrated patron of the theatre, and organized a college of actors known as the Pear Garden. (Up until recently, actors of superior merit have had conferred upon them by their fellow actors the title of Leader of the Pear Garden.)

Nearly three hundred titles have come down to us from the Sung dynasty (960-1279); unfortunately the texts themselves have been lost. Puppet shows and shadow plays are two other influential dramatic forms that are a legacy of the Sung period. It was the Yüan dynasty (1279-1368), however, that witnessed the real flowering of the theatre in China and that has been called the Golden Age of Chinese Drama. During the Yüan dynasty, China was ruled by the Mongols, and since Chinese men of letters, who normally would have held government positions, were unoccupied, they presumably found outlet for their talents in other fields. One of these was the drama, a literary form that had been traditionally or officially despised because it was considered beneath the dignity of a scholar steeped in the Confucian Classics. It is easy to see what a quickening effect such an influx of talent would have on any art form.

The Yüan plays are known by the generic name *tsa chü* or "variety plays." They contain considerable monologue and dialogue interspersed with songs that usually do not carry the plot further but are aria-like pieces; only the main character sings in any one play, although many of the characters, upon entering the stage, recite some introductory lines of doggerel. The verse form of these songs is called the *ch'ü*, a versatile poetic form that derives from the Sung dynasty *tz'u; ch'ü* were written to then existing tunes. These *ch'ü* are sometimes almost impossible to translate, but they are really the high point of a performance and, indeed, the dialogue, usually conventional and undistinguished, seems primarily to provide a context for the songs. Yüan plays contain four acts, each of which contains a song sequence employing uniform key and rhyme. Many plays, however, have what seems to be a fifth act, called a "wedge" in Chinese, usually placed before the first act but sometimes placed between two of the other acts. Sometimes called a prologue in English, it appears incorporated into the first act too; in any event, it allows the dramatist more leeway in presenting his characters and plot and has the status of a regular act except that in this "wedge" the singing part is not limited to the main actor. The most notable exception to the four-act structure of Yüan plays is *The West Chamber* (nos. **95,96**), which in its complete form contains twenty acts, a pentalogy of four-act plays. Yüan plays are of about the same length as Greek tragedies.

There is no real distinction between tragedy and comedy in Yüan drama. While the notion of tragedy is foreign to traditional Chinese drama, most plays have a serious theme, and usually the dramatic conflict is resolved by the triumph of justice either supernaturally or, as is more often the case, judicially. Preoccupation with justice may suggest that, under Mongol rule, when justice was often flung down and danced upon, the theatre was a place where wishes might be fulfilled. Certainly the drama was a vehicle for social criticism; on the other hand, there seems to be a place for comic relief in these "variety plays" and most of them incorporate some droll and even coarse humor.

Western translators have not been assiduous in producing

translations from the Yüan drama, which is, after all, the classical drama of China. Even less have they addressed themselves to the extremely long productions of the Ming and Ch'ing dynasties; Hung Sheng's *Palace of Eternal Youth* (no. **98**), an early Ch'ing play, is the only major play from either the Ming or the Ch'ing to have found its way into an English version. Rather, those writers whose interest is in Chinese theatre have almost always given their attention exclusively to the so-called Peking Opera, which came to maturity about the middle of the nineteenth century. Peking Opera is less sophisticated, less literary, but more lively than classical drama. It exists to be staged and is not intended to possess other than theatrical merit, whereas the classical plays can be appreciated now only by the highly literate. The English reader is fortunate to have available to him the numerous excellent studies and translations of Professor A.C. Scott, whose knowledge of Peking Opera is practical as well as academic.

The rise of Western-style drama in the early twentieth century came about as an attempt to reform the theatre: to substitute the vernacular language for the old-fashioned, stylized, and often incomprehensible literary language; to make drama imitate life realistically rather than artificially and symbolically; and to make drama a vehicle for progressive reform propaganda instead of for traditional Confucian morality. At first, Chinese plays were produced by student dramatic companies, but in the Western style; later, dramatic adaptations of Western works were produced, notably *Uncle Tom's Cabin*. The earliest efforts by Chinese dramatists at drama in the Western manner are largely interesting experiments, but in 1934, Ts'ao Yü's *Thunderstorm* (no. **107**) was published and produced, at last a tragedy in the Western manner worthy of comparison with the work of Ibsen (whose influence on modern Chinese drama has been considerable) or Eugene O'Neill, two dramatists whose work Ts'ao Yü admired and learned from. It is a pity that Ts'ao Yü has been so little and so poorly translated. There have been a number of modern plays translated by the Chinese of the People's Republic, but most of these have been plays written since 1949 when drama was enlisted into the services of the totalitarian Communist regime. The gain for propaganda has been the loss for art.

ANNOTATED
BIBLIOGRAPHY

Drama

91. Kuan Han-ch'ing. *Selected Plays of Kuan Han-Ching.* Tr. by Yang Hsien-yi and Gladys Yang. Peking: Foreign Languages Press, 1958. 237 pp.

This volume was produced in commemoration of the seven hundredth anniversary of Kuan Han-ch'ing, the most outstanding Chinese dramatist of the Yüan dynasty (thirteenth and fourteenth centuries), when Chinese drama was enjoying what has been called its golden age. This greatest and most prolific of Chinese dramatists was probably born about 1234, but little else is known of his life except for his plays. Study of the history of Chinese drama and dramatist is always somewhat hamstrung because drama was not, until recent times, considered legitimate literature, and so its authors were not remembered as were poets and essayists. It is, indeed, fortunate that quite a number of Kuan's plays have survived, eight of which are included in the present volume of translations.

One of the best-known plays in the collection is "The Butterfly Dream." After Mrs. Wang's husband is killed by a noble named Keh Piao, her three sons avenge their father by killing his murderer. When Prefect Pao, a famous Chinese judge, decrees that one of the sons must pay with his life, all three offer to die, and Mrs. Wang herself is told to make the choice. Because the two older boys are the sons of Wang's first wife, she decides to sacrifice her own child. When she goes to fetch his corpse, she finds him alive, for Judge Pao, under the influence of a dream, has pardoned him.

Undoubtedly the most admired of Kuan's plays is "Snow in Midsummer." The heroine of this play is Tou Ngo, who is given as a child-bride to the Tsai family to satisfy a debt. When Mr. Tsai dies, his first wife marries an old man whose son Donkey wants Tou Ngo for himself. She refuses and later when Donkey mistakenly poisons his own father, he places the blame on Tou Ngo. A thick-headed magistrate condemns her to death and there is no one to whom she can appeal. When she is led out to die she protests her innocence and prophesies that her blood will stain a white streamer on the execution ground, that there will be snow in midsummer, and that the district will suffer a three years' drought. Heaven is moved, and her prophecies come true. Her father, later appointed to high office, avenges her wrong.

Included in this volume are a study of Kuan Han-ch'ing and early woodcut illustrations of scenes from each of the plays. The translations are generally accurate but the English dialogue is somewhat stilted. The volume remains the fullest collection of Yüan dynasty plays in English.

92.   K'ang Chin-chih. "Li K'uei Carries Thorns." Tr. by J.L. Crump in *Anthology of Chinese Literature: From Early Times to the Fourteenth Century*, ed. by Cyril Birch. pp. 393–421. New York: Grove Press, 1965. (Paperback, Evergreen Book).

This play deals with some of the most famous members of a gang of robbers whose exploits were chronicled in numerous plays of the thirteenth and fourteenth centuries. It parallels almost exactly a scene in the celebrated Chinese novel *Shui Hu Chuan*, translated by Pearl Buck under the title *All Men are Brothers*, the fullest account of the Liang-shan P'o outlaws. In this play, Sung Chiang, the outlaw leader, has given his men a three-day leave, and Li K'uei, also known as Black Whirlwind, goes to a wineshop to get drunk as is his custom. He finds the shopkeeper in distress because two ruffians who passed themselves off as Sung Chiang and Lu Chih-shen, another outlaw, have kidnapped his daughter. Outraged that the leader himself should have disgraced the outlaw band, Li K'uei vows to recover the old man's daughter for him. He goes straight back to Sung Chiang and confronts him with the accusation. Sung Chiang is, of course, perfectly innocent, but Li K'uei is so sure that the two agree to bet their very heads on the matter. Sung and the other accused outlaw accompany Li down to the wineshop where Li is shocked to find that he has been mistaken. They all head back to the robber's lair where Li will have to lose his head. Meanwhile, however, the two ruffians return with the shopkeeper's daughter. While they are drinking, the shopkeeper sneaks out to tell the robbers about the two imposters. Sung Chiang agrees to pardon Li K'uei on the condition that he capture the two imposters. Li K'uei brings the two ruffians to Sung Chiang who orders that they be executed. The play ends with the honor of the robbers intact and the wineshop-keeper reunited with his daughter.

Li K'uei is essentially a comic character, and his racy speech and unusual behavior are of chief interest in this play. Professor Crump has managed the translation quite skillfully and has brought the play to life in English.

93. Li Hsing-tao. "The Chalk Circle." Tr. by Ethel Van Der Veer in *World Drama*, vol. 1, ed. by Barrett H. Clark. pp. 227-258. New York: Dover Publications, 1933.

94. ———. *The Story of the Circle of Chalk*. Tr. by Francis Hume. Emmaus, Pennsylvania and London: Rodale Press, 1954. 124 pp.

"The Chalk Circle" by Li Hsing-tao (of whom almost nothing is known), was one of the earliest of Chinese plays to find its way into a Western translation, having been translated into French by the eminent sinologist Stanislas Julien in 1832. It went through a number of adaptations, mostly German, and was the principal source for Bertolt Brecht's *Caucasian Chalk Circle*. Both of the present English versions were made from Julien's French translation but are quite reliable and readable.

The heroine, Chang Hai-t'ang, has been following the flower and willow profession in order to provide for her widowed mother. After an argument with her brother who is ashamed of her, she is married as second wife to a Mr. Ma and bears him a son. Years later, when Mr. Ma dies from drinking poison given him by his first wife, Hai-t'ang is accused of murder and taken to court. At the accusation of bribed witnesses, she is found guilty by the corrupt judge who is, incidentally, Mrs. Ma's secret paramour. She is given a new trial, however, because the details of her case have come to the attention of the famous Judge Pao. Hai-t'ang is at a disadvantage because she cannot prove that she and not Mrs. Ma is the mother of the five-year-old boy. At this point, Judge Pao has a chalk circle drawn on the floor and places the child inside it. He then instructs the real mother to lead the child outside the circle. Hai-t'ang fails twice to lead her child out and it begins to look as if Mrs. Ma is the real mother; however, when she explains to Judge Pao that she is afraid of hurting the child's arm, Pao knows who is telling the truth. Hai-t'ang is freed and the evildoers are severely punished.

95.   Wang Shih-fu. *Romance of the Western Chamber*. Tr. by S.L. Hsiung.(1935). New York: Columbia University Press, 1968. 281 pp.

96.   ———. *The Western Chamber*. Tr. by Henry H. Hart. Stanford: Stanford University Press, 1936. 192 pp.

The Western Chamber, perhaps the most celebrated Chinese play, was written by Wang Shih-fu, about whom little is known except that he flourished during the middle of the thirteenth century. The plot is taken from a short story, "The Story of Ying-ying," written by Yüan Chen (779-831), a close friend of the T'ang dynasty poet Po Chü-i. This classical tale is translated in full as an appendix to S.L. Hsiung's translation.

The plot of Wang's dramatic version is as follows: the scholar Chang Chün-jui has met Ts'ui Ying-ying at the P'u Chiu temple where she is staying with her widowed mother prior to the burial of her father. With them is a serving maid named Hung-niang. Chang falls in love with Ying-ying and, assisted by the maid, the two are able to meet at night. Mrs. Ts'ui, having promised her daughter to one Cheng Heng, is not willing to agree to the new relationship, but when they are all threatened by a robber named Sun Fei-hu who demands Ying-ying's hand, Mrs. Ts'ui offers her daughter to the one who can save them. Chang sends a messenger to a powerful friend who comes with a small army to remove the threat, but after the danger is past, Mrs. Ts'ui goes back on her word. She does, however, agree to the marriage provided that Chang successfully passes the examination that will bring him a government position. So the lovers must be separated.

In a "continuation," perhaps written by Kuan Han-ch'ing, another famous dramatist, Chang and Ying-ying are reunited after some trouble from Cheng Heng, Ying-ying's original betrothed.

Both the Hart and the Hsiung translations are excellent. Hart's version has an authoritative treatment of Chinese drama and good notes on the play and Hsiung's version has the "continuation" as well as a translation of the source story in full so that the reader can study the use which a dramatist has made of a classical tale. The reprint of Hsiung's translation further includes an excellent critical essay on the play by C.T. Hsia, whose work no student of Chinese literature can afford to overlook.

97. Ma Chih-yüan. "Autumn in the Palace of Han." Tr. by Donald Keene, in *An Anthology of Chinese Literature: From Early Times to the Fourteenth Century*, ed. by Cyril Birch. pp. 422–448. New York: Grove Press, 1965. (Paperback, Evergreen Book).

"Autumn in the Palace of Han" was the third Chinese play to make its way into a Western translation, having been translated into English under the title *The Sorrows of Han* as early as 1829 by John Francis Davis. Davis's translation is all but unobtainable now. Davis was concerned with pointing out the remarkable similarity which the play bore to Western tragedies, but so little did he regard the song sequences in the play that he neglected to translate them altogether. Difficult as these songs are for the translator, to leave them out obviously alters very considerably the character of the play, and it is fortunate that some of the plays are being translated again by scholars such as Professor Keene.

"Autumn in the Palace of Han" is the story of the treachery of Mao Yen-shou who was commissioned by the emperor to find one hundred beautiful girls from whose portraits the emperor could choose a consort. One of the girls, Wang Chao-chün, is from such a poor family that they are unable to pay the crooked minister's bribe, so he distorts her portrait. The emperor, however, has a chance encounter with her, and when he sees that she is in fact very beautiful, he orders the treacherous minister's execution. The minister, however, escapes to the Tartar Khan who is a threat to the Han empire. The false minister takes with him a real portrait of Chao-chün who is now the consort. When the Tartar Khan sees it, he agrees to withdraw his troops only upon receipt of the Lady Wang Chao-chün for himself. The emperor is forced to let her go, but she in distress kills herself. The angered Tartar Khan has the minister returned to the Han court for execution, and the enemies are reconciled and peace is restored. The triumph of justice is an almost universal theme in traditional Chinese drama.

98.   Hung Sheng. *The Palace of Eternal Youth.* Tr. by Yang Hsien-yi and Gladys Yang. Peking: Foreign Languages Press, 1955. 338 pp.

The love of the T'ang Emperor Ming for the lovely Lady Yang Kuei-fei has been celebrated by Chinese writers almost since her tragic death in 756 at the hands of rebels. One of the earliest examples is Po Chü-i's poem, "The Everlasting Sorrow," which, together with Ch'en Hung's prose version of the same story, contributed to Hung Sheng's long dramatic treatment in *The Palace of Eternal Youth,* completed in 1688 near the beginning of the Ch'ing dynasty. Lady Yang has been condemned by many Chinese writers as a woman who hastened the downfall of an empire, but Hung Sheng's theme is stated in an epilogue—"Its real meaning: true lovers who are constant/Will enjoy their love throughout eternity."

The first half of this play in forty-nine scenes details the love story from the time Lady Yang becomes Imperial Concubine until her death in scene twenty-four. Much of the second half takes place in the spirit world: Emperor Ming's love for her continues after her death as does hers for him. He sends a necromancer to search for her spirit. The Weaving Maid, one of the heavenly deities, feels pity for the two lovers and reunites them at last in the palace of the moon.

This translation is accurate, generally smooth in style, and complete except for the four-line verses that close each of the scenes in the original. The text is illustrated by a number of traditional wood engravings of scenes in the story. There is also an essay on Hung Sheng and some of the actual music that accompanies modern performances of his play.

99. Arlington, L.C. *The Chinese Drama from the Earliest Times Until Today*. (1930). Bronx, New York: Benjamin Blom, 1966, li, 177 pp.

100. Arlington, L.C., and Acton, Harold, trs. and eds. *Famous Chinese Plays*. (1937). New York: Russell and Russell, 1963, xxx, 444 pp.

These two volumes, which were originally published during the thirties and have long since become collectors' items, may be considered as companion works. A description on the title page of the first one calls it a "panoramic study of the art in China, tracing its origin and describing its actors (in both male and female roles); their costumes and make-up, superstitions and stage slang; the accompanying music and musical instruments; concluding with synopses of thirty Chinese plays." The historical survey of drama given by Arlington is informative but should be supplemented by more authoritative recent studies. The great strength of the book is its 115 illustrative plates; several are full color and foldouts illustrating scenes in plays, costumes, head pieces, beards, facial makeup, and musical instruments. Each illustration is carefully explained and Chinese character equivalents are given for all terms and names. This book is an illustrated encyclopedia of the Chinese theatre.

Famous Chinese Plays is a volume of translations and synopses of thirty-three plays from the Peking theater. The short introduction discusses fundamental stage conventions and defines a number of technical terms, many of which are used in the stage directions of the plays translated. The plays themselves are annotated and interspersed with editorial comments that explain motivations of the characters, historical context of the plays, and problems of production. There are a number of musical transcriptions as well. Of their translations, the editors write: "Since the Chinese editions are very unreliable—the language and dialogue of a single play varying in each to such an extent that only a practised eye can recognize it—we have in most cases ignored the Chap-books and given the versions as witnessed on the stage." Because in most cases no really authoritative text exists, their method seems about as good as any. At any rate, the result of their ambitious undertaking is a most instructive and entertaining introduction to the Peking theatre.

101.   Chen, Jack. *The Chinese Theatre*. London: Dennis Dobson, 1948. 63 pp.

This little book is divided into three parts, each of which treats the "three main types of theatre art in China Today." The first is the classical theatre which, being the least familiar to the Western reader, occupies almost two-thirds of the book. It is a most concise and instructive essay, indeed as informative as anything of comparable length in the English language. Chen discusses such topics as theatre origins, make-up, costumes and props, music, character types, and gestures. The text is illustrated by ink drawings of props, musical instruments, and the layout of a Chinese playhouse. The second part deals with Western-style theatre in China from about 1915, when student dramatic companies began to produce such works as *Uncle Tom's Cabin* and *La Dame aux Camelias*, until the thirties, when Chinese dramatists such as Ts'ao Yü began writing plays in the Western manner that were worthy of comparison with the works of O'Neill and Shaw. The "Yang ko theatre" is the third type of theatre art that Chen discusses. Yang ko was originally a kind of folk dance performed "at the time of field labour." As cultivated now, it "is a modern folk art theatre imbued with the most modern and revolutionary ideas of world culture." This book is to be recommended to the beginning student of Chinese drama because it is both concise and comprehensive in its coverage of contemporary Chinese drama.

102. Alley, Rewi. *Peking Opera: An Introduction Through Pictures.* Peking: New World Press, 1957. 101 pp.

As explained in the preface to this volume, the text has "really been written to accompany the so human pictures that Eva Sias has taken of Peking Opera as a living, real part of Chinese life." There are pictures here, all large, many in full color, which depict many sides of Chinese theatrical life: student actors in training, actors making up, a variety of theatrical costumes, musical performers, and actual scenes from plays. These latter are close-up shots and are an interesting and illuminating accompaniment to the introductions to the ten plays from which they were taken. There are short chapters on the training of actors and on the various roles as well as on costumes. There is also a sketchy survey of Chinese drama which, like many Chinese Communist publications, is more polemical than instructive: Alley's main point seems to be that the drama has always been a vehicle for social criticism, feeding the revolutionary fervor of the Chinese common man. Be that as it may, the government of the People's Republic seems to have encouraged the continuance of this traditional art, and the present volume is as good an illustrated introduction to its subject as can be had.

103. Scott, A.C. *The Classical Theatre of China.* New York: Barnes and Noble; London: George Allen & Unwin, 1957. 256 pp.

104. ———. *An Introduction to the Chinese Theatre.* New York: Theatre Arts Books, 1959, 92 pp.

105. ———. *Mei Lan-Fang: Leader of the Pear Garden.* Hong Kong: Hong Kong University Press, 1959. 140 pp.

106. ———. tr. *Traditional Chinese Plays.* 2 vols. Madison: University of Wisconsin Press, 1967-69. 165 and 156 pp.

It must be borne in mind from the beginning that by "Classical Theatre of China," A.C. Scott does not mean classical Chinese drama, the drama that enjoyed its golden age during the thirteenth and fourteenth centuries. He concentrates on that Chinese drama, of comparatively recent development, which in the West is often called Peking Opera and in Chinese is called *Ching hsi* (Peking drama). In *The Classical Theatre of China*, Scott furnishes his readers with a somewhat informal sketch of the development of drama in China up until the *Ching hsi* came to maturity; the bulk of the book, however, is given over to a discussion of certain technical aspects of *Ching hsi* itself, such as the music, the various roles, acting technique, and the plays themselves. Of particular help is the long chapter on the technique of the actor, which discusses such topics as costume, makeup, and body gestures and movements. In *An Introduction to the Chinese Theatre*, Scott has done much the same thing except that, designed as it is for the general Western reader, he has cut technical discussion to a minimum and has devoted most of his book to an appreciation of twenty typical and well-known Chinese plays. Both books include illustrations by the author as well as a number of photographs.

Mei Lan-Fang is a biography of one of China's leading actors, the greatest of female impersonators. It offers a unique view of Chinese theater in its informal treatment of the early training and long career of the man whose name, during much of this century, has been nearly synonymous with Chinese theatre.

The two volumes of *Traditional Chinese Plays* contain two plays from the repertoire of the Peking theater and two plays from the somewhat earlier *K'un-ch'ü* or K'un-shan Drama. The introduction to the volumes survey Peking and K'un-shan drama, respectively, and each of the four plays is supplemented by considerable discussion of the problems of staging, costume, and character. A number of photographs illustrate scenes from the play as performed by Chinese and Western actors. A.C. Scott is perhaps the foremost Western student of and spokesman for the traditional Chinese theater (as distinguished from the history of Chinese drama), and anyone interested in the production of Chinese plays cannot afford to overlook his several studies and translations.

107. Ts'ao Yü. *Thunderstorm*. Tr. by Wang Tso-liang and A.C. Barnes. Peking: Foreign Languages Press, 1958. 183 pp.

108. ———. *Sunrise: A Play in Four Acts*. Tr. by A.C. Barnes. Peking: Foreign Languages Press, 1960. 189 pp.

109. ———. *Bright Skies*. Tr. by Chang Pei-chi. Peking: Foreign Languages Press, 1960. 127 pp.

110. Chen, David Y. "The Trilogy of Ts'ao Yü and Western Drama." In *Asia and the Humanities*, ed. by Horst Frenz. pp. 26-37. Bloomington, Indiana: Indiana University Comparative Literature Committee, 1959.

Ts'ao Yü, whose real name is Wan Chia-pao, is perhaps the leading dramatist of modern China. Born in 1910, he made his debut as a dramatist with *Thunderstorm*, the first part of a trilogy and first produced in 1933. The other two parts of the trilogy are *Sunrise* (1936) and *The Wilderness* (1937), the latter of which is not available in English translation. *Thunderstorm* is almost without question the most formidable play in the Western manner to have been produced in China, even though, as its author knows well, it is much too long and thickly melodramatic at times. Heavily indebted to Western tragedy from Aeschylus to O'Neill, Ts'ao Yü's play came as a shock to his countrymen and still has considerable power even today.

Thunderstorm deals with the decline of a traditional patriarchal family in the early part of the present century. The head of the family, Chou Pu-yuan, is living with his second wife and two sons, the elder of whom, Chou Ping, is his son by a previous marriage. Chou Chung, the younger son, is his son by Fan-yi, his present wife. From an early point in the play, it is suggested that there has been an illicit affair between Chou Ping, the older son, and Fan-yi. There are two servants in the Chou household: Lu Kuei, a worthless lout whose chief abilities are drinking and bowing and scraping to those he considers to be his betters, and his daughter, Ssu-feng, who is three months pregnant with the illegitimate child of Chou Ping. The Lus are expecting the arrival of Lu Ma, Ssu-feng's mother, who has been away from them working elsewhere. When she arrives, she discovers that she is at the home of the man who wronged her years before and turned her out while she was with her second child. It turns out that she is the mother of Chou Ping as well as of Ssu-feng and another son, Lu Ta-hai, a worker at the mine owned by Mr. Chou. When Fan-yi discovers Chou Ping's plans to go away with Ssu-feng, she reveals the sordid story of her earlier affair with him. Gradually, it comes out that Ssu-feng is bearing her own brother's child and when she learns of it, she rushes out into the night and is electrocuted by a fallen wire which had been neglected during the day. Chou Ping takes a revolver into the study and kills himself.

Thunderstorm points up the corruption of traditional Chinese society by showing how the sins of individuals are visited upon their children. *Sunrise* focuses on the sick society as a whole represented by the many types who come into contact with an upper-class prostitute, Chen Pai-lu, the central character of the play. *Bright Skies,* written in 1954, five years after the establishment of the People's Republic of China, is interesting only because it shows Ts'ao Yü as a propagandist in contrast to the earlier Ts'ao Yü as a dramatist. It has to do with the liberation of a medical college from the clutches of an American imperialist doctor who, as it is later revealed, has had a woman murdered so that he could have her bones as specimens. Such conflict as the play contains is resolved when the last of the Chinese doctors hears about American germ warfare in Korea and is convinced of the evil of the Americans. In *Thunderstorm* Ts'ao Yü created an impression of doom hanging over the Chou family; in *Bright Skies* the only impression is of the paranoia of the main characters.

These three plays are in complete translation except in *Thunderstorm* where the long prologue and epilogue are missing. The translations are accurate but shoddy, having been made with little regard for colloquial naturalness. The tired style of *Bright Skies* seems somehow appropriate, but it is a pity that the translations of *Thunderstorm* and *Sunrise* are as generally poor as they are. Ts'ao Yü deserves better. The essay by Professor David Chen is to be recommended because of its brief but informed treatment of Western-style drama in China and its discussion of Ts'ao Yü's trilogy and its indebtedness to the works of Western dramatists.

111. Kuo Mo-jo. *Chu Yuan*. Tr. by Yang Hsien-yi and Gladys Yang. Peking: Foreign Languages Press, 1955, 124 pp.

Kuo Mo-jo, who was born in 1892, has been one of modern China's most versatile and prolific men of letters. He was one of the early poets in the vernacular, has made numerous studies of ancient China and the Chinese language and has written much about politics and modern history. His play *Chu Yuan* was written in 1942.

Ch'ü Yüan was a celebrated poet who lived during the Warring Kingdoms period (fourth century B.C.). He was a loyal minister of the southern state of Ch'u and repeatedly warned his sovereign King Huai against any alliances with the treacherous and powerful state of Ch'in. In this play, Chang Yi, the prime minister of Ch'in, and Chin Shang, another Ch'u minister, conspire to discredit Ch'ü Yüan in the eyes of King Huai so that the latter will turn against Ch'ü and favor the party which seeks the Ch'in alliance. Ch'ü Yüan is talking with King Huai's treacherous queen when she suddenly cries out, accusing him of having made improper advances. The stupid king is taken in completely, and Ch'ü Yüan is out of favor at court and believed by everyone to be mad. His pupil, a girl named Chan Chuan, alone remains true to him, and she discovers the treachery of the queen. She is arrested for her knowledge, but a sympathetic guard takes pity on her and frees her. She runs to Ch'ü Yüan who is to be killed, and when she reaches him exhausted, he unwittingly gives her poisoned wine that had been intended for him. She dies, but Ch'ü himself is enabled to escape. Tradition has it that Ch'ü Yüan drowned himself after seeing his state come to ruin, but presumably a suicide is not a proper example of loyalty and right thinking.

Kuo Mo-jo is a Ch'ü Yüan scholar of some stature, and his play is based upon Ch'ü's poems, biographical accounts of Ch'ü and, of course, his own fertile imagination; it is an interesting reconstruction of a man, the many details of whose life are obscure. It is by no means a contemptible example of modern Chinese drama, and the translators have produced a readable and accurate English version.

112.   Lao Sheh. *Dragon Beard Ditch*. Tr. by Liao Hung-ying. Peking: Foreign Languages Press, 1956. 99 pp.

Dragon Beard Ditch is of interest as an example of socialist realism in contemporary Chinese drama because of its author, who was, before 1949, a leading literary figure in China. Lao Sheh is the author of a number of novels and short stories, the best known of which, at least to Western readers, is translated under the title *Rickshaw Boy*. The first act of this three-act play takes place in 1948, and describes the sad plight of a group of people who live beside a stinking ditch in Peking. Their lives in such a dangerous and unsanitary environment are further threatened by both the thoroughly corrupt Nationalists headed by Chiang Kai-shek, "the biggest crook of them all," and thieving gangsters led by a Pekingese Al Capone named Black Whirlwind. If the gangsters don't steal their wares at market, the government taxes them to death. The last straw is the death of a little girl who has fallen into the ditch and drowned.

The rest of the play takes place after the "liberation," that is to say after the establishment of the People's Republic of China. People are happier, they begin to get jobs they were unable to obtain before, their enemies are slowly being put out of commission and, last of all, the people's government repairs the terrible ditch and transforms the disease-ridden slum into a park.

Characters are of two kinds, good and bad. Of the good characters, some seem to have sympathized with Communism almost since birth; some others need to be convinced, and their ultimate conversions, because not instantaneous, are supposed to seem plausible. The bad characters are just bad. One cannot resist the urge to quote a few lines from the ballad which, except for shouts of "long live Chairman Mao," close the play:

To all you people, I joyfully state,
The People's Government is truly great.
Is truly great, for it mended the Ditch,
And took great pains for us though we're not rich.

INDEX

Authors, editors, translators, and titles given in each numbered entry are all presented below in a single alphabetic listing. Please note that the usefulness of this index is limited: persons and titles referred to in the body of the annotations and in the introduction are not indexed. Since this bibliography is arranged chronologically and by topical groupings, the incompleteness of the index, the general editor hopes, is justifiable.